LSAT Guide

Contents

1

The Test

Prospective students have a lot of questions about the test and about law school. In this section we're going to explain some of the basic things that you might want to know.

1.1 - LSAT F.A.Q.

Should I go to law school?

That depends, are you comfortable with a lot of reading and writing? Do you enjoy debating and arguing (as in making and defending reasoned assertions, not throwing the dishes at your girlfriend/boyfriend/roommate/younger brother)? A legal education is narrower than what you encountered in college and is mostly focused on teaching you a set of skills - critical reading, analysis, synthesis, and presentation of a wide range of information, as well as advocacy, counseling, and negotiation. Do you have any experience of an actual legal environment and do you think it's something you would be comfortable in as a career? Ultimately going to law school is a personal choice.

How do I register for the test?

You'll need to register on the LSAC (the people who run the LSAT) website and to do that you'll have to create an account. The test is held at various testing centers in your town (high schools, colleges, etc) and you should register as early as possible so that you can get the test center that is most convenient for you since space is limited and the longer you wait the more likely it is that you'll be left with a test center that is far away or inconvenient for you.

When should I take the test?

The short answer is that you should take the test whenever you've prepared enough for it to do as well as you can. The LSAT is held four times a year - in June, October, December, and February. Most law schools will require you to take the test by December if you want to enroll in the fall of next year (ie if you want to go law school in the fall of '12 you need to take the test by December of '11). However, most law schools also have rolling admissions which means that by the time you submit your application they will already have accepted people into their program and there will be less space. You should check with the schools you're applying to if admission is rolling. LSAC score reports are held on file for five years so you don't have to apply to law school immediately after you take the test, you can apply at any point in the five years after you take the test.

Can I take the test more than once?

Yes, however you're limited to three tests in a two-year period. So you *can* take the test more than once, but that doesn't necessarily mean that you *should*. LSAC releases your entire score report to any schools that you apply to, and that includes all of the tests that you've taken - not just the latest one or the one with the highest score. Some schools will average your scores together and will only pay more attention to the higher score if it's substantially higher. You should check with the schools that you're applying to for more details. In general, I tell my students that they should aim to do their best the one time that they take the test.

What's on the test?

The test consists of five 35-minute multiple choice sections. Of those five only four are going to be scored and one of the sections is an experimental section in which LSAC tests out questions for future tests. You won't know which section is the experimental section.

The test is designed to measure the skills that are considered essential for law school: reading comprehension of complex texts, making inferences from information, critical thinking, and reasoning/argument analysis. To that end, the test is broken down into three distinct parts: an analytical reasoning (games) section which measures your ability to understand a structure set of relationships and to draw logical conclusions about it, two logical reasoning (arguments) sections which measure your ability to analyze and evaluate arguments as they're found in normal speech and writing, and a reading comprehension section which measures your ability to read and understand/evaluate lengthy and dense materials like you would find in law school. In addition, there's an unscored writing sample, also 35 minutes, which is sent to the law schools that you apply to. The first three sections are given one right after another, with a 10 to 15 minute break after the third section.

What's a good score?

That depends on a couple of different factors, and the short answer is that obviously the higher the better. But, the key thing is that you need to keep in mind what schools you're applying to. The test is scored on a scale from 120 to 180 with no deductions for wrong answers and no section being given more weight than any other section. Your LSAT score and your GPA are the two most important elements in your law school application; the essay, letters of recommendation, work experience/etc are all much less important than when you were applying to college. If you're applying to the top 10 or 15 schools then you'll need to do well on both. Take a look at this website for a good analysis of what kind LSAT score you're going to need in order to be competitive for the school that you're aiming for. If you don't feel that you did well on the test you can cancel the score on the day of the test or via written request within the first six days after the test.

So how do I prepare for this thing?

The LSAT is a skill test, not a knowledge test. What I mean by that is that there is no particular information that you need to study and memorize. Primarily you're tested on your reasoning abilities. 'Reasoning abilities' is a broad term but the important elements are those identified above - the ability to comprehend complex texts, make inferences/deductions, and think critically. The fact that the LSAT is a skills test structures how you should approach preparing for it. In a nutshell: you need to learn the strategies that will allow you to most effectively approach all the different question types in the test (different question types have different approaches) and you need to practice those strategies until you've got them down cold. The way to do that is to work on specific question types in isolation and with no time pressure - at this stage you're just working on getting the questions right and on internalizing the approach for each one.

The videos in my lectures are designed to dissect variations for each of the question types and to provide a step-by-step approach for each one. In this ebook I also provide tips and explanations for each question type as well and I give you a list of questions for each of the question types. Once you have the question types down for a section you should move on to doing full sections in isolation. The order that I teach starts with the logic games section, followed by arguments, followed by reading comprehension. The reason for this is that games stress skills that are useful for arguments and reading comprehension, and arguments likewise stresses skills that are useful for reading comprehension. Once you're comfortable with the approaches to the different question types and have practiced the sections in isolation you should move on to doing timed tests. Ideally, by the time you're ready to take the test you should have done every single LSAT that's been published. Roughly, the breakdown would be the first 30 for practicing and internalizing the techniques and the last 30 for doing timed tests. Keep this 3-part structure in your head:

- you first need to learn the correct techniques and approaches

- you then need to internalize the correct techniques and approaches

- finally you need to apply what you've learned under time pressure

Take a look at the rest of this ebook for information specifically covering the different parts of the test to get a better idea of what you're in for. Then feel free to check out my website lsat.totaltestprep.net for more information and if you've got any specific questions you can always send me an email, I try to answer as many as I can. I have over 20 hours of animated lectures covering the entire test and I do tailored one-on-one online tutoring (via a real-time audio/video virtual classroom). I offer every potential student a free information session where we talk about the student's goals/possibilities/etc and where I explain the test and studying for it in a bit more depth. This information session is in addition to the free first class that covers conditional reasoning. So if you want a more detailed chat about the LSAT, a set of in-depth instructional videos, or are thinking of getting tutoring, feel free to drop by my site!

2

Studying for the Test

The LSAT is like any other test. If you want to do well on it, you have to study. But, different exams test different things and the LSAT is completely different from the majority of exams that you may have encountered in your academic career. The LSAT doesn't test what you know, so there's no way to cram for it; it tests your abilities - *reasoning abilities* to be specific - and as with any other ability or skill you improve through practice. The saying is 'practice makes perfect', but more accurately it's 'practice makes permanent, perfect practice makes perfect'.

In order to improve the sort of skills that the LSAT tests, you need to learn essentially two things: the right approach for each question type, and how to effectively apply those approaches so that you'll be as accurate as possible on test day.

In this chapter we'll deal with learning to effectively apply the correct approach to each question type. The remaining chapters in this ebook will deal with the specific question types that you'll come across in the test. Here we will also go over:

- general study habits

- specific studying strategies for the three sections

- a schedule that provides you with an optimal approach and is best suited for your situation

2.1 - General Study Habits

Effective studying

I'll repeat it once again, the LSAT doesn't test your knowledge, it tests your skills. An exam that tests your *knowledge* will require you to either learn specific concepts or information. For example, whether you remember how to reduce fractions, or what the significance of the French Revolution was. An exam that tests your *skills/abilities* will not require you to learn and remember any information, instead it will use problems to gauge how well you *do* something.

Perfect practice

So, you're not studying to learn information, you're practicing to improve a skill. With that in mind, you'll need to accept is that it's going to take time. Depending on your capacities and how much information you needed to learn you could've learned everything you needed to know for that Econ mid-term in two weeks, maybe a week if you're pretty smart. It just doesn't work that way for the LSAT. There is going to be an unavoidable amount of repetition involved before things start to 'click'. Think of riding a bike. In general a reasonable minimum for someone that can dedicate between 15 to 20 hours a week to the test would be around 3 months of intense studying. A more optimal schedule would require 4 to 5 months. With that in mind here are some additional effective study habits that you'll need to incorporate if you want to do well on the test.

- **Study when you're at your optimum**. What you do at home/in the library/etc with a prep test is what's going to happen on test day in the test center. Remember, the point isn't simply to learn something, it's to train yourself and improve your performance. Whatever you repeat on a regular basis is what you're going to be left with. If you study for the test when you're tired and unable to concentrate then you're not going to magically do well on it even if you're well-rested and concentrated on test day. So you need to pick a time where you can approach your studying with a fresh mind. A lot of my students make time in the morning before work or class, and if you're a morning person then this can work very well for you. I was never a morning person, my best work was always at night. If you work full-time or can't schedule a morning study session a couple of common-sense suggestions can be very helpful. Take a quick nap when you get back from work; even if you have a hard time getting up in the morning it generally won't be as difficult to set your alarm for half an hour or 45 minutes and get up when it rings. Avoid sitting in front of the TV/internet when you get back in from the office because that can get pretty distracting pretty quickly. Likewise, simply meditating can be a good way of re-focusing and re-energizing.

- **Be consistent with your study time.** Pick a particular time and place and do your studying then and there. Studying for an hour every day is much better than studying for 10 hours straight once a week. If you create a routine you'll find that it's much easier to stick to it for an extended period of time, and of course, like I keep mentioning, the very thing that this exam tests is something that is developed through repetition over an extended period of time. And 10 hours once a week isn't going to help. Having a routine will also make it much easier for you to maintain the kind of schedule that you'll need to follow in order to cover everything on the exam. Also, you don't necessarily have to study every day, 5 or 6 days of studying with one day of rest and relaxation will probably be more effective and less likely to cause you to burn out.

- **Create an effective studying environment.** Your studying environment is very important as well. An uncluttered, comfortable desk and chair will help you focus and will be most like what you will encounter on test day. Try to have your study materials organized and accessible at your desk (or wherever you choose to study) as well as pencils, timers, etc. Also, don't study somewhere where you'll be easily distracted, and if you have roommates or a spouse try to work out a schedule where you know that you won't be interrupted for the amount of time that you'll be working. Working at the local coffee shop may seem like a lot of fun in the commercials but it's a terrible idea in real life, particularly for this test. Remember, a big part of what you're doing requires well-developed focusing skills and that's not something that is produced in a noisy Starbucks.

- **Do things outside of studying that help you learn.** There are a couple of things that have been shown to be very helpful in terms of intelligence and studying efficiency that it would be very useful to integrate into your overall approach.

  - physical exercise - research has shown that moderate aerobic physical exercise (brisk walking/light jogging) for 45 minutes 3 times a week can be very beneficial. If my students already go to the gym I definitely encourage them to continue and if they don't I recommend it to them.

  - meditation - meditation has likewise been shown to be very beneficial for its cognitive benefits. Meditation is known, and has been used for a long time to help with focus and concentration, something that is central to this test. There are a lot of places on the net that you can find information about meditation but for the purposes of the LSAT a simple and basic breathing exercise can be very helpful. The way you would do it would be to sit or lie down comfortably and close your eyes. Then, simply start to pay attention to your breath as you inhale and exhale. Do this for 15 minutes (you may want to start out at 5 minutes and gradually build up to 15 minutes or even 30 minutes); the point is to try and pay attention only to your breath. You will find your attention wandering every so often, gently bring it back to your breath. You may also do it by counting your breath and paying attention to the numbers, starting over every time you lose count.

○   cognitive games - there have been some promising results with programs and video games that purport to increase your intelligence and working memory. The most significant so far is a type of game that's called 'dual n-back' where the object is to try and memorize strings of letters and numbers. On the useful links page I've provided links to a version that you can download for free along with other cognitive training games. Spending ten to fifteen minutes a day with these games may turn out to be a good investment of your time.

Ok, so keep these points in mind as you're putting together your goals and strategies for doing well on the test.

2.2 - Specific Section Strategies

As I've mentioned the LSAT is a skills/ability test and your studying needs to reflect that. In this chapter we'll talk about the common approach running through all three sections and the variations for each particular section. Basically there are three key things that structure how you will approach each section and studying for the test as a whole:

- you need to learn the correct approaches for each question

- you need to internalize the correct approaches for each question

- you need to be able to do the section under time pressure

The games section

You should start studying this section first because the skills that you develop in this section carry over well into the other two sections and the overall experience works better than if you were to do this section third or fourth. The approach I teach, and which I think is the most effective approach for the games, doesn't require you to make any deductions and instead places a lot of emphasis on the questions in each game and less emphasis on the actual game where you're presented the scenario. Since you're not making deductions you don't have to know all the different varieties of scenarios and the different deductive strategies that would provide you with a lot of information before you even took a look at the first question.

The first thing that you need to learn for the games section are the basic elements that are common to every game scenario and the standard ways of diagramming games. You would then practice this by simply diagramming the games and rules from the first 10 tests without paying attention to the questions. Once you have a good idea of the basic structure of the scenarios in the games and standard ways of representing it and the rules in diagram form you would move on to the questions. The approach to doing the games correctly rests on making and using test diagrams to evaluate the answer choices. In order to do that there is a different step-by-step procedure for each of the different question types. Learning and practicing these procedures is what will take up the bulk of your time in this section. You'll do that by learning the actual procedure for a particular question type and then practicing it on every example of that type in the first 10 tests. You'll do this for each question type and the goal in this phase of your LSAT studies is simply to get a good grasp of the procedures and to be able to do them consistently, without worrying about time constraints. The next phase, which overlaps with studying for the arguments and then reading comprehension section, is to first combine everything you've learned and do whole games, and then the phase after that is to do whole games under time pressure.

The arguments section

This section comes after the games section since the games section is a good introduction to conditional reasoning and abstract thinking in general. The arguments section will take the bulk of your studying for the LSAT because it has the most concepts and question types that need to be learned and because, more so than the games section, improvement is a function of simply spending a lot of time doing the arguments and building an intuition concerning what the right answer is. There are quite a few question types in the argument section and the approach to doing well on them is based on learning the specific procedures for each one and learning why the correct choice is correct and the incorrect choice incorrect.

The first thing that you'll need to do is to learn the correct approaches for each of the different question types. Take the question types one at a time and learn the approaches for each variation. Then practice doing the questions until you're comfortable doing them before moving on to the next question type. The basic strategy here is similar to what you did for the games. Once you learn the approach for a particular question type and its variations go through the first 10 tests and do every example of that question type. By the time you finish the questions from the first 10 ten tests for each question type you'll have internalized the approaches and procedures for them and will have a solid foundation. The next phase is to combine everything you've learned about the different question types and do entire argument sections. This will overlap with your studying for the reading comprehension section.

The reading comprehension section

This is the final section that you will be studying. The reasoning skills that you developed in the arguments section are going to be very useful for the reading comprehension section because you can think of the passages in the reading comp section as extended arguments. You'll be reading the passages for structure, not for content and so being able to analyze and evaluate the key points and support for them is critical. Likewise, a significant portion of the questions that you'll encounter in this section will be identical to question types from the arguments section. Reading comprehension, unlike the arguments and games sections, is more of a skill that's developed over a longer time period but there are certainly approaches that are more effective and that can be learned. Likewise, there are also specific strategies for the different questions.

The first thing that you need to do is practice your comprehension of the passages. To do that you'll need to study my approach that consists of understanding and paying attention to the four key things that are found in every passage. And then you'll need to go through every single passage in the first 10 tests plus the double passages from a couple of the later tests so that you get accustomed to approaching the passages so that you're specifically reading for structure. Once you're done with that you can move on to the specific question types. Unlike the arguments section where it made sense to do each question type in isolation here it makes more sense to learn the approach for each question type first and then simply to do the passages, practicing the questions as you come across them for that passage. So here you'll go back to the passages from the first ten tests that you already read through and this time around you'll do the questions. Once you're done with that you'll be prepared to integrate everything and start doing full tests under time pressure.

Putting it all together

Once you're done with the reading comprehension section you're ready to move on to doing entire tests under time pressure. The way that you should have broken down your studying for each section you should have done all of the first ten tests a part at a time, first the games, then the arguments, and then the reading comp. And likewise you should've been doing individual sections of the games from the next ten tests as you were studying for the arguments and reading comp, and individual sections of the arguments from the next ten tests as you were studying for the reading comp. Basically, at some point you should have about 30 preptests left and have done the previous published preptests question by question and section by section. Now you're going to move on to do the rest of the preptests under timed conditions; this is where most of the improvement will occur. Try and do a test a day, and it's equally important to review what you got wrong so that you'll be able to see where you're making your mistakes. This entire process should ideally take you up to two or three days before test day. The few remaining days before the test should be spent relaxing and not worrying about the test. And then finally, rock the test!

2.3 - Potential Self-Study Schedule

This schedule presents the breakdown of how you should prepare for the test in terms of the sequence that you should follow. The amount of time that it takes you to finish everything depends on the individual but the standard amount of time it generally takes is between three to five months. I've arranged the studying here in terms of sessions that incorporate studying and practicing particular concepts.

session 1 - conditional reasoning	HW
go over the different variations in conditional reasoning that you'll encounter on the test, use the videos from lecture 1	exercises from lecture 1

session 2 - games scenarios	HW
study the information for dealing with games scenarios, either lecture 2 in the videos or in the resources section	diagram the games from the first 10 tests but only the scenarios and the rules, leave the questions for the next sessions

session 3 - games questions 1	HW
study the approach for the potential arrangement, arrangement can be true, and can be true questions	do those questions from the first 10 tests, there's a list of them at the end of the ebook

session 4 - games questions 2	HW
study the approach for the must be false, must be true, and can be false questions	do those questions from the first 10 tests, there's a list of them at the end of the ebook

session 5 - games questions 3	HW
study the approach for the list, greatest/smallest, and possible diagram questions	do those questions from the first 10 tests, there's a list of them at the end of the ebook

session 6 - introduction to arguments	HW
study lecture 6 in the videos or the article in the resources section that introduces arguments	do the games section from test 21

session 7 - arguments questions 1	HW
study the approach for the conclusion, weaken, and strengthen questions	do those questions from the first 10 tests - there's a list of them at the end of the ebook, and do the games section from test 22

session 8 - arguments questions 2	HW
study the approach for the assumption, logical conclusion, and evaluate questions	do those questions from the first 10 tests - there's a list of them at the end of the ebook and do the games section from test 23

session 9 - arguments questions 3	HW
study the approach for the principle (justify), and principle (scenario) questions	do those questions from the first 10 tests - there's a list of them at the end of the ebook, and do the games section from test 24

session 10 - arguments questions 4	HW
study the approach for the inference, can't be true, and formal logic questions	do those questions from the first 10 tests - there's a list of them at the end of the ebook, and do the games section from test 25

session 11 - arguments questions 5	HW
study the approach for the paradox, and disagreement questions	do those questions from the first 10 tests - there's a list of them at the end of the ebook, and do the games section from test 26

session 12 - arguments questions 6	HW
study the approach for the method of reasoning, flaw in the reasoning, and parallel reasoning questions	do those questions from the first 10 tests - there's a list of them at the end of the ebook, the arguments sections from tests 21 – 23, and the games section from test 27

session 13 - reading comp single passages	HW
study the concepts dealing with perspective, opposition, tone, and structure, either in lecture 13 or in the resources section	analyze the reading passages from the first 10 tests, and do the arguments sections from tests 24 – 26

session 14 - reading comp questions	HW
study the approaches to the single passage questions	do those questions from the first 10 tests, the arguments sections from tests 27, 28, and the games section from test 28

session 15 - reading comp dual passages	HW
study the approaches to the dual passage questions	do those questions from tests 52 – 56

session 16 - tests
tests 29 - 34

session 17 - tests
tests 35 – 39

session 18 - tests
tests 40 - 44

session 19 - tests
tests 45 - 49

session 20 - tests
tests 50 - 54

session 21 - tests
tests 55 - 59

session 22 - tests

tests 60 - 63

This is the standard sequence that you need to follow in order to get the most out of your studying. Remember, when you're doing the homework it's equally important to review what you got wrong or what you weren't sure about after you're done as it is to actually do it. By reviewing you're developing an understanding of the criteria that LSAC uses for the correct and incorrect answers and that will make it easier for you to pick the right choice. Also, the real improvement will happen from session 16 on, when you start doing tests under timed conditions. The more tests you do and the more you review your mistakes, the better you will do on the actual test.

3

Conditional Reasoning

Conditional reasoning is a very important part of the test. It's a type of reasoning that deals with a specific type of relationship between at least two things and it features prominently throughout the test, the games and arguments sections in particular. Lecture 1 goes over it in detail and is freely available so take a look at the videos and do the exercises.

I won't go over conditional reasoning in depth in this ebook because my videos are freely available online.

What is it?

The basic idea is that conditional reasoning is a type of reasoning and it's very important for the test. Simply put, conditional reasoning deals with a specific relationship between two (or more) things. The relationship is that if the first thing is true, then the second thing has to be true. In other words, the second thing can't be true without the first being true. Take a look at this example:

> **If you're in school, then you're a student.**

Here the first part is *'if you're in school'* and the second part is *'then you're a student'*. This sentence is called a **conditional statement** and it doesn't actually tell us that anyone is in school, or that anyone is a student. All it's telling us is that if we know that someone's in school, then we know that that person is a student. So the basic point is that conditional reasoning deals with conditional statements, which are statements that present a specific relationship between at least two things. In this case being in school, and being a student.

Where is it?

In other words, how do we know that we're dealing with conditional reasoning. Well, if you look back to the example above you'll see that the first part of the conditional statement starts with the word *'if'* and the second part starts with the word *'then'*. The words 'if' and 'then' are indicators that let you know that you're dealing with a conditional statement. There are other words that accomplish the same function and this is an important element of learning conditional reasoning that's covered in detail in the animated video lectures.

Also, where is conditional reasoning found in the test? It's found all throughout the test; for example, a lot of the rules in the games section are presented as conditional statements and it's very important to understand exactly what is meant by those statements and what you can deduce from them. A lot of the arguments in the arguments section, as well as parts of the reading comprehension passages likewise rely heavily on conditional reasoning and there it's important to understand how conditional reasoning figures in the larger context of an argument or a passage and what it means for the validity of a conclusion.

So, take a look at the conditional reasoning lessons page on my website and make sure to go through all of the videos and to do all of the exercises. These videos are free to everyone and are designed to provide the prep work for my first tutoring session with a potential student. I always have a free lesson with any potential students so that they can see how my tutoring works and what the animated videos look like. So please feel free to check out the site!

4

Logic Games

The analytical reasoning section, also known as the games section, is one of the three types of LSAT sections and along with the reading comprehension type it only appears once on the test. Of course, the experimental section can be an analytical reasoning section, but only one of them would be scored. The games section is designed to essentially test how well you can understand and draw conclusions from a structure of relationships, and the rationale for this is that this skill set is similar to what lawyers and law students need to have when confronted with legal problems.

The section consists of four 'games' that contain a passage that looks like a brain teaser or brain puzzle followed by between 5 and 7 questions each. Each passage is a scenario that presents a group of persons, places, things, or events and is followed by a set of rules that describe the relationships in that group. So for example a simple version of a scenario might be that horses A, B, and C win first, second, and third place in a race and the rules might say that horse A isn't last, that if horse B wins first then horse C gets third, etc. This scenario is then followed by questions that ask you pick the correct choice based on the info given. The questions may simply ask you to draw a conclusion simply based on the information in the scenario and rules or they may add additional conditions, ie: if horse A is second then in what place is horse B? A less frequent question variation is where one of the rules is temporarily suspended.

Doing well on this section requires you to understand precisely what the scenario and the rules are saying, but the passage is designed to be clear and not tricky or ambiguous. Everything you need in order to answer the questions correctly is presented in the passage and questions, you shouldn't introduce any of your own assumptions.

This section is difficult for several different reasons. First, the relevant information is presented in awkward and unnatural language; unlike the arguments or reading passages where you're given information in a form that's roughly similar to something you would read in everyday life here it's formal and stylized. Second, you're asked to keep track of the information and the relationships between the relevant elements; complexity is always challenging. And third, it's intimidating because you're asked about things that aren't even presented in that information; you're going to be making deductions and coming to conclusions based on the relationships in the passage. The way that we'll deal with these difficulties is first to present you with concepts that will help you quickly comprehend what the scenario and rules are saying and to organize that information most effectively and then to show an effective procedure for each question type that completely reduces your need to depend on deductions.

In this chapter we're going to present some basic information about diagramming the logic games, keeping track of the rules, and basic information about the questions.

4.1 - Diagramming the Games

Here is a very simplified game of the type you will encounter on your LSAT:

> Five horses, A, B, C, D, and E are racing at the racetrack. The horses finish in first to fifth place.
>
> - Horse E has to come after horse A.
>
> - Horse C can't be last.

Like all the other games on the LSAT, the game above is composed of three parts:

- The scenario, which tells us the who, what, where and when. In the above example, that would be the part that says "Five horses, A, B, C, D, and E are racing at the racetrack. The horses finish in first to fifth place".

- The rules, which give you additional information. In the above example, the rules are that horse E has to come after horse A, and that horse C can't be last.

- The questions, which you have to answer, and which are based on the scenario and the rules.

Movable and Structural Elements

Let's take a look again at the scenario for the above simple game:

> Five horses, A, B, C, D, and E are racing at the racetrack. The horses finish in first to fifth place.

The five horses are examples of the movable elements while the places that they finish in are examples of the structural elements. Movable elements are simply those things that you move around and whose grouping, or order, you can change. Structural elements are those things that provide a position for the movable elements. **Your first task when diagramming a game is figuring out which elements are movable and which ones are structural.**

Sequential Games

In the game above, there are many different possible arrangements for the five horses. For example, the order that the horses finish the race could be A, D, B, E, C, or it could be D, C, E, A, B, or it could be B, A, E, C, D, and so on. Because we're changing the sequence of the letters but keeping the basic structure that 1st place is first from the left, 2nd place is second from the left, etc., this game is what is called a **sequential game**. That is, it's a game where you have to put the elements in the correct sequence.

You need to keep that in mind as you're going through this logic game so that you'll have an easier time making a diagram that will help you do the questions and test the answer choices. **In order to make diagrams, the basic process is to isolate the movable and structural elements and to draw spaces above the structural elements where you'll insert the movable elements.** For this game it would look something like this:

_ _ _ _ _

1 2 3 4 5   ABCDE

Here's an example of the other major type of game:

> Horses A, B, C, D, E, and F are in either farm 1 or farm 2.
>
> Three horses are in farm 1 and three are in farm 2

This would be a good way of diagraming it:

```
1   2      ABCDEF

—   —

—   —

—   —
```

Once again, the horses are the movable elements and the farms are the structural elements. But, notice that in this case our diagram is not telling us which horses are next to one another, but rather which horses are grouped together. In other words, this structural variation **groups** together the movable elements, and hence this is a grouping game. In addition to the grouping games there's a third major variation which is a combination of these two that we just went over. I call it the sequential-grouping game, and it's basically a combination of the sequential and the grouping type.

Understanding games scenarios is crucial to doing the games correctly. If you keep in mind that there are really only three types of games (sequential games, grouping games, and sequential-grouping games) and if you diagram those games accordingly, you'll be well on your way to acing the games section.

4.2 - Keeping Track of the Rules

Why the games have rules

Rules are statements that provide additional information about how the elements in the game interact with one another. Furthermore, the rules add details about the relationships between the elements. **The basic function of the rules in any of the LSAT logic games is to provide constraints on the number of possible arrangements.**

Types of rules

Here's our simplified game from before:

> Five horses, A, B, C, D, and E are racing at the racetrack. The horses finish in first to fifth place.
>
> - Horse E has to come after horse A.
>
> - Horse C can't be last.

There are three basic types of rules:

Rules that relate the movable elements to one another – In the game above, the rule that "horse E has to come after horse A" is an instance of this.

Rules that relate movable elements to structural elements – In the game above, the rule that "horse C can't be last" is an instance of this.

Rules that relate structural elements to one another – These types of rules appear more often in the grouping games. For example, consider the following game:

> Horses A, B, C, D, E, and F are in either farm 1, 2, or 3

If a rule for that game said "if farm 1 has 2 horses then farm 3 has 2 horses", that would be an example of the third type of rule.

Why the rules are important

The rules are important because they guide you to what has to be true and what can't be true. You'll be checking them when testing your answer choices, so, you should symbolize the rules with representations that are easy to both make and understand.

Rules for the sequential games are going to provide you with more details about the positions of the movable elements either relative to one another or relative to the structural elements. So you might be told that horse A is after horse C, or that horse A is two spots before horse E. Or, you might be told that horse A can't finish third. This is an example of a movable element being specified in relation to a structural element. I tell my students that when they're presented with a rule that specifies the location of a movable element in relation to a structural element then they should add that element directly to the structure. In this case you would put an A right underneath the 3 and cross it out. (because A **can't** be in third place)

Rules for the grouping games likewise give you details about the movable elements relative to one another and to the structural elements. In this case the difference is of course that it is not the sequence but rather the association of elements to one another that is important. So you might be told that horse A can't be on the same farm as horse B, or that horse if horse C is on farm 1 then horse D is on farm 1 as well. The basic information that these rules give you is whether certain movable elements are or are not found together, or whether they can or cannot go in a certain group. Conditional reasoning appears more frequently for these types of games, as shown by the last example. For the sequential-grouping games you'll have examples of the same basic rules since the games themselves will deal with both sequence and grouping.

How to keep track of the rules

You should try to symbolize the rules using a consistent system that makes sense to you. Numbered dashes for the structural elements and letters for the movable elements are common and effective symbols. Whatever you settle on, if you're able to internalize that system, this will help you do the games a lot more quickly and accurately on test day. Furthermore, if you have clear representations of the rules, that will be a lot of help when making arrangements to test out your answer choices.

4.3 - The Questions

The questions are completely covered in the online videos. The basic principle is to use test arrangements to evaluate the answer choices. A test arrangement is simply a diagram where you put the movable elements into the structural elements in such a way so that none of the rules are broken. Each question type has a specific step-by-step process that allows you to most efficiently see which of the answer choices is the correct one. I won't cover the approaches in-depth in this ebook because it's actually a very simple and mechanical system that's very easy to learn (I need to eat to, can't give *everything* away). Here I'll introduce you to the different question types and their basic information.

Can be true questions

These are the most common questions and should be done first. Common keywords that let you know that you're dealing with this question type are:

can be true, could be true, must be false EXCEPT, can't be true EXCEPT

For this question type you're asked to pick the answer choice that can be found in a working arrangement. The correct answer won't conflict with any of the rules and the incorrect answer will be in conflict. Basically you're making arrangements to try and find the correct answer. There's a particular variation to this question which is generally found right after the scenario where you're presented with answer choices that are complete arrangements.

Must be false questions

These are also a very common question type and should be done right after the 'can be true' questions. Common keywords are:

can't be true, isn't possible, can be true EXCEPT

These questions ask you to pick the answer choice that can't be found in a working arrangement. The correct answer will be in conflict with some of the rules and the incorrect answers won't be in conflict. Basically you're making arrangements to try and eliminate the incorrect answer.

Must be true questions

These questions are likewise very common and should be done after the 'must be false' questions. Common keywords are:

can't be false, can be false EXCEPT

Here you're asked to pick the answer choice that will be found in every appropriate working arrangement; the correct answer won't be in conflict with any of the rules and the incorrect answers will be in conflict. Basically you're making arrangements to try and eliminate the incorrect answer by trying to make a working arrangement with the negative of each answer choice.

Can be false questions

This is an uncommon question type; these questions appear fairly rarely and should be done after the 'must be true' questions. Common keywords are:

could be false, must be true EXCEPT, can't be false EXCEPT

These questions ask you to pick the answer choice that can't be found in any appropriate working arrangement. The correct answer will conflict with some of the rules and the incorrect answers won't be in conflict. Here you're basically making arrangements to try and find the correct answer by once again making a negative of the answer choice.

List questions

This is also a less common question type, though it's more common than the 'can be false' questions, and it should be done after it. Common keywords are:

complete and accurate list

'List' questions ask you to pick the answer choice that gives you a list of elements (either structural or movable) that meet some sort of criteria. The correct answer will have all the elements that meet that criteria and the wrong answer will either not have all of them or have some that don't meet the criteria. You do these questions by essentially making arrangements to see which choices have too many or not enough elements.

Greatest/smallest

These are actually two separate question types that are similar in approach. 'Greatest' questions, and 'smallest' questions. They're also a less common type and should be done after the 'list' questions. Common keywords are:

what is the minimum ..., what is the maximum ..., what is the earliest ..., what is the latest ...

The 'greatest/smallest' questions ask you to pick the answer choice that gives you the correct number of elements that meet some sort of criteria. The choices will always be numbers in ascending order and the correct answer will be that number of elements that meets that criteria. You essentially do these questions by testing away from the extreme answer.

Possible arrangements

This is the final question type and is likewise fairly rare; these questions should be done after the 'greatest/smallest' ones. Common keywords are:

In how many distinct ways can we ..., how many different diagrams ...

The 'possible arrangement' questions ask you to pick the answer choice that gives you the correct number of possible arrangements that you can make given a specific condition. The correct answer will be that number of arrangements that can be made. Essentially do these questions by making as many arrangements as you can.

Ok, so those are the different question types. One thing to keep in mind is that every question in the games section will either be a condtional question or not. The conditional questions simply preface the question with added information, for example: *'if horse A is in farm 1 then which of the following can be true?'* This is a conditional 'can be true' question. You should always do all of the conditional questions first in the order that's presented above (conditional can be true, then conditional must be false, then conditional must be true, etc) and then do the remaining ones in the same order (any remaining can be trues, then must be false, etc). The reason for that is because a big part of the approach I teach rests on having previous test arrangements that you use to identify correct choices and eliminate incorrect choices and this order maximizes your efficiency.

Conclusion

We've just covered the different aspects of the logic games that you'll need to know in order to do well on that section. The approach that I teach doesn't depend on making deductions from the rules before you attack the questions. Instead, it focuses on simple and mechanical steps for each of the different question types. You're basically making test arrangements in order to eliminate the wrong answer or identify the correct answer. I didn't present detailed information about the actual steps that you need to follow for the questions because it's a very learnable and simple system. The videos on my site go over all of the different question types and explain how to do them in full detail. Likewise I have interactive exercises that go over dozens of questions along with detailed video explanations of several different games that cover all of the major variations that you'll find in the scenarios and rules. My tutoring sessions focus on attacking each question type in isolation first so that my students develop a sound understanding of the approach and then we go through full-length games. Please check out my site lsat.totaltestprep.net for more information.

5

Arguments

The arguments sections will always be at least two of the five sections on the test, if the experimental section is an arguments section then you'll have three, with two being scored. The basic skill that this section tests is your verbal reasoning, ie your ability to deal with arguments as they're presented in ordinary language, how well you comprehend, analyze, and evaluate them. The rationale behind this is that as a lawyer what you're fundamentally doing is arguing *for* something *against* someone.

These sections consist of 25-26 short passages, about a paragraph in length - generally no longer than four or five sentences - followed by a question, sometimes two. The passages may or may not be arguments and the questions will ask you something designed to test your abilities to think and reason critically. We'll be going over each of the different question types and their variations in this section.

Doing well on this section depends on you paying attention to the meaning of the key elements in the passage and in the answer choices.

These sections are difficult for two basic reasons. One, critically approaching an argument is not a trivial and obvious skill. You need to be taught to recognize the structure of an argument and analyze and evaluate it; is it good/bad?, what's unstated?, what's implied?, etc. And on this test you need to be able to do that well. And two, this kind of critical reasoning is taxing and energy-consuming in and of itself. Just reading something to sound out the words in your head is one thing, but reading it so that you know what you've read is another, and reading it so that you know what you've read and have critically evaluated it is yet another level of difficulty and mental commitment. The way that you'll do well on these sections is by first learning what the different question types are and the best way to approach them, and then by practicing as many questions as possible so that you internalize that approach and develop your intellectual stamina to handle two sections under time pressure.

5.1 - Argument Fundamentals

Every argument question (otherwise known as a "logical reasoning" question) on the LSAT has three parts. It has a "passage" which gives you the relevant facts. The passage is followed by the "question", which you have to answer. And then below the question you have the "answer choices", from which you chose the correct answer. I will use this terminology in this and all subsequent articles concerning arguments.

What is an argument?

Please take a look at the pairs of sentences below:

> **A bike is a healthy, energy-efficient means of transportation. Bikes have been in use since the early 19th century.**
>
> **I got a flat tire on my bike. Therefore, I won't ride my bike to school tomorrow.**

While both of these pairs of sentences are about bikes, they are different in a fundamental way. The first is simply a collection of statements while the second is an argument. But what is it about the second pair of sentences that makes it an argument? If we look at the first pair we see that the two sentences are solely descriptions of bicycles. The two sentences provide two facts about bicycles, but the two facts aren't related in any meaningful way.

However, the second pair of sentences ARE related in a meaningful way. The second sentence ("I won't ride my bike to school tomorrow.") is something the author wants you to believe, while the first sentence ("I got a flat tire on my bike") is the evidence for believing that. And that's simply what an argument is, *it's a collection of statements where one statement is something that the author wants you to believe and the other statements are reasons for supporting that belief.*

Conclusions

What the author wants you to believe is commonly called a "conclusion". **The first thing you need to look for in any LSAT argument is the author's conclusion.**

Generally, an argument has one main conclusion, and the way that you locate it is by looking for conclusion-indicators. Those are words that let you know that what's going to follow them is a conclusion. For example, the word "therefore" in the argument above is a conclusion-indicator. Here are some other conclusion-indicators that are commonly found on the LSAT:

thus, as a result, in conclusion, consequently, it follows that, accordingly, it shows that, for this reason, hence, so

In other words, if a statement says, "thus, we should lower the voting age to 15", most likely that statement is the conclusion of that argument. Or, if a statement says "it follows that the new prescription drug doesn't work", that too is most likely a conclusion. The above list isn't exhaustive but it is a good idea to become familiar with it so that you'll be able to quickly identify the conclusions of arguments.

Premises

The sentences that support the conclusion of an argument are called "premises". **Once you find the conclusion of an argument, the next thing you have to look for are the premises that support that conclusion.**

Generally, the arguments on the LSAT have multiple premises, and the way that you locate those premises is by looking for premise-indicators. As with conclusion-indicators, premise-indicators are words that let you know that what follows is going to be a premise. Consider the following argument: "Since I got a flat tire on my bike, I won't ride my bike to school tomorrow." Here the very first word in the argument is a premise-indicator, the word 'since'. Below are other examples of premise-indicators:

because, given that, due to, for, as can be seen by, the reason being, in that

You will find arguments with any combination of these indicators and as you can see from the examples given it's perfectly legitimate to have an argument where you have neither premise-indicators nor conclusion-indicators. The indicators aren't required for there to be premises and conclusion, they're merely there to help you. If you don't have indicators, a useful way of figuring out which is the premise and which is the conclusion is to place a conclusion-indicator in front of a sentence that you think is the conclusion and to see if that makes sense, or if it sounds logical. If so, then that's your conclusion, and if not, then try putting a conclusion-indicator in front of another sentence.

Argument Structure

Let's go back to our original argument:

> **I got a flat tire on my bike. Therefore, I won't ride my bike to school tomorrow.**

This argument is about as simple as they come. There is one conclusion (the second sentence), and one premise (the first sentence). However, most of the arguments on the LSAT will be significantly more complicated. For example, conclusions and premises don't have to be separate sentences, they can also be parts of sentences. And not only that, they don't have to be in any specific order. In general, the premises tend to come before the conclusion but it's also common to see the conclusion first, and the LSAT tries to trick you at times by having a tricky arrangement where the conclusion actually comes in the middle, in between the premises. It's not position that determines whether a statement is a premise or a conclusion but rather the relationship that the statements have to one another, so essentially you have to pay attention to what's acting as support and what's being supported.

Or, take a look at this example:

> **I won't ride my bike to school tomorrow because I got a flat tire on my bike. As a result, I'll be late to class.**

This is similar to the previous argument that we've been working with but it adds something important. The first part of the first sentence is the conclusion while the second part of the first sentence (the part starting with "because") is a premise. But the second sentence is an additional conclusion that uses the conclusion from the first sentence as support: I won't ride my bike to school tomorrow and as a result I'll be late for class. "I'll be late for class" is the overall conclusion of the argument and "I won't ride my bike to school tomorrow" is an intermediate or sub-conclusion. It's a conclusion that acts as support for the main conclusion. And this is something that you'll have to pay attention to as you're going through the arguments because it's a common structure that you'll encounter. There's no reason to get anxious, just keep in mind that because you've spotted conclusion-indicators or you recognize that a statement is being supported by other statements, that doesn't mean that you're dealing with the main conclusion. In fact, you can have arguments with multiple sub-conclusions that support a main conclusion.

In addition, as you're going through the arguments, keep in mind that you should also pay attention to what is unstated. For example, in the biking to school argument we've been working with, there's an assumption that the author will be late unless he or she bikes to school. And likewise there's the implication that he or she won't be riding back home from school (if you don't ride to school then you can't ride back). Obviously you can't know everything that's unstated but you will have to pay attention to logical gaps, since those will prove to be important for a lot of the questions.

The most important thing for handling the arguments is being able to follow precisely what is presented and knowing what the premises and conclusion are. Keep in mind that the actual arguments will often include information that isn't directly related to the premises and conclusion, and those arguments will usually be more complicated. But, the basic structure of premises and conclusion will be there and that's what you'll need to pay attention to.

5.2 - Conclusion Questions

The "conclusion" question type appears regularly in every test, often not more than twice per section and usually towards the front and middle. This question type tests your ability to recognize arguments, since the ability to figure out whether a statement is a premise or conclusion is something you need to have in order to evaluate arguments. You can tell you're doing a "conclusion" question if you're asked something like the following:

"Which one of the following is the main conclusion of the argument?", "Which one of the following provides a logical completion to the passage?", "Which one of the following most accurately expresses the main conclusion drawn in the argument?", etc...

Each conclusion question type contains a passage that can be either an argument or just a collection of statements. If it's an argument then that argument will not be clearly presented and you won't be able to easily tell what the premises are and what the conclusion is. If it's just a collection of statements (all premises, no conclusion), then one of the answer choices will be the the most reasonable conclusion that can be drawn. Furthermore, all the premises in the passage will provide support for one of the answer choices.

EXAMPLE

In order to be environmentally-friendly, most publishing houses print books on recycled paper. But, it's probably a better idea for them to start publishing e-books. E-books have a minimal impact on the environment since they're only responsible for the energy that goes into running the computer system.

The main point of the argument is that

> **A) The way that publishing houses can be most environmentally-friendly is to stop publishing books printed on recycled paper.**

> **B) Publishing houses need to publish more books on cd.**

> **C) It's a better idea for publishing houses to start publishing e-books than to print books on recycled paper.**

In the above case you should be able to see that there are no obvious premise and conclusion indicators. However, you should also see that the third sentence, "E-books have a minimal impact on the environment..." supports the second, "...it's probably a better idea for them to start publishing e-books." Likewise, the first sentence merely presents a fact but the second sentence is an evaluation – it suggests something. The first sentence presents context and background info and the second sentence is the main conclusion in the argument. So with the knowledge that we have the conclusion we now need to go through the choices and find the one that most closely resembles it.

Choice A is not the correct answer because it says something that isn't mentioned at all in the passage. Saying that publishers should publish more e-books and saying that publishers should stop publishing print books are two very different things. They may seem similar on a superficial reading but in fact this choice adds new information and is wrong. **Any time you see new information on a conclusion question answer choice you can safely know that the choice is incorrect.**

Choice B is not correct because it's subtly different from what the actual conclusion says. The conclusion doesn't say that more books on cd need to be published, it says that more e-books need to be published, and those are two different things. The difference is subtle but it's a difference, and in fact this is a common wrong answer choice as well. **Whenever you are presented with a choice that subtly shifts the meaning of a key term, you need to train yourself to be on the lookout for that** because it's going to be important for most of the rest of the question types as well. Pay attention to the meaning of key concepts and whether that meaning shifts from the content to the answer choice.

Choice C is correct because it basically restates what we determined to be the correct choice. And in those variations of the conclusion question type where the argument does contain a conclusion the correct choice is simply going to restate it.

So that's the basic approach that you need to take when doing these question types. Now take a look at this example for a common variation:

> **Businesses that don't replace outdated technology won't remain competitive in the marketplace. LaserTech hasn't installed a new computer inventory system in over three years, and new systems come out once a year.**
>
> **The main point of the argument is that**
>
> **A) A business that doesn't replace outdated technology won't remain competitive in the marketplace.**
>
> **B) LaserTech will definitely go out of business.**
>
> **C) LaserTech won't remain competitive in the marketplace.**

This is another simplified version of a conclusion question and it illustrates the second major variation that you'll find for this question type. As with the previous example the first thing that you should do is analyze the content to see if you can find a conclusion. And here we don't have any premise and conclusion indicators, the relationship between the sentences is that the first presents a general rule and the second is an example of a situation where a condition for the general rule is fulfilled. And you can't say that either sentence supports the other.

So in these situations you're looking to see if there's a conclusion that the argument is pointing towards. The first sentence presents a general rule that says that something will happen if a condition is met, and the second sentence says that there's a specific situation where that condition has been met. So we can see that the argument is moving towards the conclusion that LaserTech won't remain competitive in the marketplace. And **this is an example of the argument type where two premises work together to support a conclusion**. So we have a potential conclusion and let's go through the answer choices to see if we can find it.

Choice A is incorrect because it simply restates one of the premises. You need to be on the lookout for this since it's a common incorrect answer. In particular, this can be tricky in those situations where the restated premise is a sub-conclusion, that's a bit trickier since it's a conclusion – just not the main conclusion.

Choice B is incorrect because there's a shift and because it uses extreme language. The argument isn't talking about anyone going out of business, it's saying that business will no longer be competitive, and those are two slightly different things. Likewise, the answer choice says 'definitely', which is an adjective that conveys certainty. **Any time**

that you have an adjective that has that kind of unqualified certainty whether it's definitely, always, never, etc then you should be suspicious of it since most arguments aren't so black and white.

Choice C is the correct answer because it combines the two premises in the argument and articulates the logical conclusion. Businesses that don't replace outdated technology won't be competitive, LaserTech is a business that hasn't replaced outdated technology, so LaserTech won't be competitive.

That's the basic approach to these conclusion question types. The question will ask you to choose the conclusion that restates the actual conclusion in the argument or that is the most appropriate and reasonable conclusion give the information in the passage. You need to look for premise and conclusion indicators and try to figure out the basic structure of the argument. Correct choices will either restate the conclusion (which won't be obvious) or will be a logical conclusion to the premises in the passage. Incorrect answers will add new information, have a shift in terms, use extreme language, or restate one of the premises.

5.3 - Weaken Questions

The '"weaken" question type tests your ability to evaluate argument strength and appears regularly on every test, often several times per section. When you weaken an argument you give reasons to be skeptical about the conclusion. To that end, the correct choice is going to introduce information (most of the time new information) that will undermine the support for the conclusion, and the incorrect choices are either not going to be relevant or will actually make you believe the conclusion even more. You can tell you're doing a "weaken" question if you're asked something like the following:

"The argument would be most seriously weakened if which one of the following were discovered?", or "The argument would be most seriously weakened if which one of the following were discovered?", or "Which one of the following, if true, most seriously weakens/undermines the argument?", or "The reasoning in the argument is most vulnerable to criticism because it fails to consider the possibility that ...".

If you noticed, the word "argument" appears in every one. The reason is that in order to weaken an argument, you need to have an argument that you can weaken. The passage is always going to be an argument, but that doesn't mean that it will be an obvious argument. In fact part of the difficulty in doing some of these questions comes from the fact that it's not always evident what the premises are and what the conclusion is.

EXAMPLE

The army ant is going to become extinct because the parts of the Amazon where it lives are going to be cleared away.

The argument would be most seriously weakened if which one of the following were discovered?

> **A) The army ant only lives in the Amazon.**
>
> **B) Logging in the Amazon has slowed down in recent years.**
>
> **C) Army ants thrive in rainforest areas in Asia and Africa.</i>**

This is a simplified version of a weaken question. In order to do this question type we have to identify the premises and conclusion, and as well, we have to be aware of the unstated assumptions in the argument. In this case of the example argument above, the first part of the sentence is the conclusion and the second part is the premise. Red army ants are in danger of extinction because their habitats in the Amazon are in danger. But we need to critically examine how the argument moves from the premise to the conclusion. Just because their habitat in the Amazon is in danger does that mean that the army ants are going to become extinct? What if they don't only live in the Amazon and they're not in danger in their other ecosystems? What if they can move from that place in the Amazon that is going to be cleared to another place in the Amazon that isn't in danger? What if they can adapt to the place once it's been cleared? Etc.

The premise talks about the ants' habitat in the Amazon being in danger and it has to make a lot of assumptions to get from that to the conclusion that the ants are in danger of extinction. That's the basic approach: pay attention to what the conclusion is saying and what's being used to support it, in this case army ants' habitat is going to be cleared vs. army ants everywhere are in danger of extinction. Keeping this in mind, let's go through the answer choices.

Choice A is incorrect because it actually strengthens the argument. If army ants only lived in the Amazon that's more reason for you to believe that clearing their habitat would be a problem. This is a type of wrong answer choice that is relatively common and is tricky because it's relevant to the argument – just in the opposite way – and if you're not paying enough attention you may pick it by mistake.

Choice B is incorrect because it's irrelevant. Just because logging has slowed down doesn't mean that there's less reason to believe the army ants are going to become extinct. This choice is tricky because it may seem to be attacking one of the premises – that the army ants' habitat is going to be cleared – but it's not actually saying that, it's saying something subtly different. Maybe the logging hasn't slowed down in areas where the ants live, or maybe their habitat is going to get cleared, only more slowly. Keep in mind, the wrong choices don't necessarily have to strengthen the argument – they could simply be irrelevant.

Choice C is the correct answer because it addresses one of the assumptions that's made to get from premises to conclusion, that the army ants live only in the Amazon. This choice brings up information that shows that assumption is not true. If there are army ants outside of the Amazon, and those ants are not in danger then the fact that the army ants in the Amazon are in danger isn't enough to conclude that army ants in general are in danger of extinction. **And this is basically what the correct answers for**

the weaken questions will look like, they will bring up information that questions an unstated assumption needed to get from the premises to the conclusion.

In addition, you'll find weaken EXCEPT questions with some regularity. These are questions where you're also given an argument but where the question asks you for the answer choice that *doesn't* weaken the argument. Four of the answer choices are going to weaken the argument and one isn't. The really important thing to remember here is that the correct choice isn't necessarily going to have to *strengthen* the argument, it's just going to have to *not weaken* it. So it could be irrelevant as well.

Ok, that's the basic explanation of and approach to doing these questions. Make sure to have a good grasp of what the premises and conclusion are and to analyze the connection between them, in particular thinking about unstated information that can be questioned; pay attention to the subtle shifts in the concepts used in the premises and the concepts in the conclusion.

5.4 - Strengthen Questions

The "strengthen"' question type tests your ability to evaluate argument strength and appears regularly on every test, often several times per section. This type of question is very similar to the "weaken" question from the previous pages, only of course the difference is that the correct answer choice in a weaken question makes the conclusion less likely, while the correct answer choice in a strengthen question makes the conclusion MORE likely. Common ways of asking the question are:

"Which of the following would most strengthen/support the argument?", "Which one of the following, if true, most strengthens/supports the argument?", "The reasoning in the argument would be most strengthened if which one of the following were true?", etc.

EXAMPLE

Listening to classical music while you study helps you study better. You should listen to Mozart while studying for your chemistry final.

Which of the following would most strengthen the argument?

> **A) Mozart was a well-known amateur chemist.**

> **B) It is very difficult to study the history of classical music.**

> **C) Numerous scientific studies have confirmed that listening to classical music while doing something increases your focus and concentration.**

This is a simplified version of a strengthen question. In order to do this question type we have to identify the premises and conclusion, and as well, we have to be aware of the unstated assumptions in the argument. In the above argument, the first sentence is the premise and the second is the conclusion. The conclusion is a recommendation to apply the general principle stated in the premise.

The next step is to look for unstated information that connects the premises and conclusion and to keep in mind how any additional information might make the conclusion more likely. In this case the premise talks about "classical music" and "studying better" while the conclusion talks about "Mozart" and "studying for the chemistry final". Maybe the music helps but only if you've been doing it for a while, or maybe it doesn't work if you have to study intensely for something like a final. The basic thing is to have a good idea of what exactly the premises are saying and what the conclusion is saying. Keeping this in mind, let's go through the answer choices.

Choice A is incorrect because it brings up irrelevant information. Whether or not Mozart was a well-known amateur chemist doesn't give us additional reasons to believe that we should listen to Mozart while studying for the chemistry final. In this answer choice, you're presented with something that combines various bits of information found in the argument so that the choice sounds relevant but in actuality has no bearing on the validity of the argument. This is a standard tactic for wrong choices.

Choice B is also incorrect for the same reason. It too is irrelevant. This one is difficult though because it seems to be talking about the relevant concepts: "studying" and "classical music". However, there's actually a subtle shift; the choice says that it's difficult to study the history of classical music, meaning that it's difficult to study classical music as a subject, but the argument talks about studying WHILE listening to classical music. This is another example of a common wrong answer choice: **subtly using the key terms in a different way from the way they are employed in the argument itself.**

Choice C is the correct answer; it provides additional information that gives us more reason to believe the support. The premise asserts that listening to classical music while studying is beneficial and the choice provides evidence that gives us reason to believe that classical music is beneficial and that illustrates how it would be beneficial. A lot of correct answer choices will be like this, that is, **they'll present additional information that gives reasons to believe one of the premises or they will justify a premise through an illustration or example.**

That was one type of argument, take a look at this example:

Journalists shouldn't make up facts for a story. Ann-Marie made up facts in the concert story and therefore she broke a code of journalistic ethics. As a result, she should be fired.

Which one of the following most supports the argument?

A) Ann-Marie didn't make up any facts she simply failed to reveal her sources.
B) If journalists don't have the facts then they shouldn't report on a story.
C) Reporters who break a code of journalistic ethics should be fired.

Ok, so evaluating the argument the first two sentences are premises and the last sentence is the conclusion. If you notice there's a subconclusion in the second sentence: 'Ann-Marie broke a code of journalistic ethics', the support for that is the she made up facts in the concert story. Looking at our argument we see that there's a gap between the premise in the middle sentence and the conclusion. All the premise tells us is that Ann-Marie broke a code of journalistic ethics, but the conclusion is that she should be fired. That gap needs to be bridged with an additional premise that connects the two, something that says that if someone breaks a code of journalistic ethics then they should be fired. So we'll keep that in mind as a potential answer and we'll go through the answer choices.

Choice A is incorrect because it brings up information that actually weakens the argument. It provides additional evidence that questions the premise that Ann-Marie made up facts. If she didn't make up facts then she shouldn't be fired on the grounds that she made them up. Once again, this is a wrong answer choice that appears with some frequency. In the weaken questions wrong answer choices would strengthen and here in the strengthen questions wrong answer choices will weaken. However, as before, just because the correct choice will strengthen the argument that doesn't mean that the incorrect choices will weaken it.

Choice B is incorrect because it's not relevant, the argument doesn't talk about whether or not journalists should report on a story but on whether or not they should be fired if they make up facts. These wrong answers are tricky because they seem to be talking about something related to the argument but actually they're not relevant at all. Just because they deal with the concepts from the argument doesn't mean that they're relevant, you have to pay attention to exactly what they conclusion says and exactly what supports it.

Choice C is the correct because it provides the bridge between the premises and the conclusion. It presents information that allows us to tie together the info in the premise – breaking journalistic ethics, with the info in the conclusion – being fired. And this is an example of the other major type of variation in the strengthen question type, where the argument isn't strengthened by additional information that gives us more reason to believe a particular premise, but where a key assumption that ties together information (generally premise to conclusion, but sometimes from premise to premise) is made explicit.

Ok, the basic approach to doing these questions is to have a good grasp of the argument, to consider ways that additional information can provide support, and to pay attention to unstated information that helps get from the premises to the conclusion.

5.5 - Assumption Questions

The "assumption" question types appear regularly in every test, often several times per section. These questions test your ability to evaluate the relationship between the premises and the conclusion; they are somewhat similar to the "strengthen" question type. Common ways of asking the question are:

"Which one of the following is an assumption required by the argument?", "Which one of the following is an assumption on which the argument depends/relies?", "The argument requires that which one of the following be assumed?", etc.

You'll notice that the word "assumption" is in each question variation. An assumption on the LSAT is an unstated premise that HAS TO BE TRUE in order for the conclusion to be true. In other words, if you think that a certain answer choice is the assumption in an argument, it should be impossible for you to think of a situation where that answer choice is false while the conclusion remains true. So, if you need to check whether an answer choice is an assumption in an argument, you need to try to think of a scenario where that answer choice is false but the conclusion is still true.

You will find two major assumption variations on the test, and here we'll cover the first one.

EXAMPLE

> **The Giant Red centipede has a bite that is as toxic as that of the Black Widow spider. So we can say that the Giant Red centipede has a dangerous bite.**
>
> **Which one of the following is an assumption required by the argument?**
>
>   A) **The Giant Red centipede kills many people every year.**
>
>   B) **The Giant Red Centipede is more dangerous than the Black Widow spider.**
>
>   C) **The Black Widow spider has a dangerous bite.**

The first thing that we need to do is establish a clear picture of the structure of the argument. In particular, we need to locate the gaps between the premises and the conclusion. Here the first sentence is the premise and the second sentence is the conclusion; the centipede's bite is as toxic as the spider's, therefore the centipede's bite is dangerous. There doesn't seem to be any obvious new information in the conclusion that isn't in the premise but when we look at it more closely we see that there's a shift. The premise is talking about how the centipede's bite is as toxic as the spider's whereas the conclusion says that the centipede's bite is dangerous. All we're told in the premise is that the two bites are equally toxic, but what if the Black Widow spider doesn't have a very toxic bite? What if its bite isn't dangerous at all? We need to make an assumption that the spider's bite is toxic enough to be dangerous. So with that in mind let's go through the choices.

In order to check whether Choice A is the assumption, you have to try to think of a situation in which choice A is not true, that is, the Giant Red centipede does not kill many people every year, while the conclusion remains true, that is, the centipede has a dangerous bite. For example, maybe the Giant Red centipede could have a very dangerous bite but not kill many people every year. Perhaps it lives somewhere where there are virtually no people and although just about everyone who gets bitten dies, that number is very low, say 5 or 10 people per year. Therefore, A is not an assumption the argument makes because it does not have to be true in order for the conclusion to be true.

This is an important difference to keep in mind between the "strengthen" questions and the "assumption" questions. The correct choice in an assumption question won't simply make the conclusion more believable, the correct choice will have to be true in order for the conclusion to be true. And what we did is a good way of checking if the choice is an assumption; you should negate the answer choice and check to see if that's compatible with the argument. **If you can have a scenario where the choice is false and the conclusion is still true then you know that choice is not the assumption.**

Choice B is tricky but it's incorrect as well. Once again, in order to check if this answer choice is the assumption, we should try to think of a situation in which choice B is not true, that is, the Giant Red centipede is not more dangerous than the Black Widow spider, while the conclusion remains true, that is, the centipede has a dangerous bite. For example, we could have a scenario where they are equally toxic and equally deadly. Since B does not have to be true for the conclusion to be true, it too is not an assumption the argument makes.

Choice C is the correct answer since it closes the gap between the premises and conclusion by presenting information that bridges the shift. If the centipede is as toxic as the spider, and the spider has a dangerous bite, that means that the centipede is also deadly. And negating the choice we get 'the spider doesn't have a dangerous bite' which will make our conclusion impossible since if the centipede's bite is as toxic, but the bite isn't toxic enough to be dangerous then the centipede doesn't have a dangerous bite. So to sum up, if you negate an answer choice, and that makes the conclusion impossible, you've found your assumption.

That was one of the main variations for the assumption questions, and it's similar to some of the strengthen questions since you're looking to link up the premises and conclusion by closing a logical gap. But take a look at this example:

> **Sven studied very hard for the LSAT. So Sven will do well on the LSAT tomorrow.**
>
> **The argument requires that which one of the following be assumed?**
>
> **A) Sven did all of the practice LSATs.**
>
> **B) Sven improved quite a lot from the first time that he took the LSAT.**
>
> **C) Sven won't fall asleep in the middle of the test tomorrow and sleep through two sections.**

As with the previous example we first need to establish a clear picture and look for logical gaps or shifts in meaning. The first sentence is the premise and the second sentence is the conclusion. And there is a gap that can be bridged; the premise talks about studying hard and the conclusion talks about doing well. So we could say something along the lines of 'anyone who studies hard will do well on the test'.

Choice A is incorrect because it's not an assumption. It doesn't close the gap and although it probably strengthens the argument that Sven will do well on the test it doesn't necessarily have to be true. We can envision a scenario where Sven didn't do all of the practice LSATs but he did most of them and he studied intelligently enough to have all the relevant concepts and tactics internalized. As we discussed in the previous article, **if you can think of a scenario where the choice is false and the conclusion is still true then you know that choice not the assumption.**

Choice B is also incorrect because it too is not something that closes the logical gap or that has to be true. Maybe Sven didn't improve a lot but he improved 5 points from a

170 to a 175 and his entire improvement came in a section that was difficult for him and that he studied almost exclusively.

Choice C is the correct choice. This is the second major variation for the assumption question type and it's unlike the previous one because it isn't an assumption that closes a logical gap. Instead, choice C is simply something that has to be true in order for the conclusion to be true. The way that the LSAT generally frames these types of answer choices is by presenting a potential problem for the conclusion and then showing that it's not a problem. So in this case if Sven were to fall asleep and miss two sections then there's no way that he could do well on the test. And the answer choice states that's not true, so it removes it as a potential problem. We could check by negating the choice and we'd see that there's no conceivable scenario where Sven falls asleep and does well on the test. Another way that the LSAT presents these answer choices is by simply pointing out something that has to be true but that is generally overlooked. For example another correct choice could read "Sven will take the test".

That's the basic explanation of and approach to the "assumption" questions. When doing them keep in mind that there are two basic variations – where you close a logical gap and where you choose something that has to be true, usually something that's shown not to be a potential problem. Remember, these questions aren't like strengthen questions in that they don't just make the conclusion more likely, but they're also necessarily true.

5.6 - Logical Conclusion Questions

The "logical conclusion" question type appears regularly in every test, often several times per section. For these questions you're going to be looking to bridge the logical gaps, generally between the premises and the conclusion. Common ways of asking this question are:

"The conclusion of the argument follows logically if which one of the following is assumed?", "Which one of the following, if assumed, allows the argument's conclusion to be properly drawn?", "Which one of the following does the most to justify the conclusion?", etc.

If you are having trouble finding the bridge between the logical gaps, then you can use the following strategy:

You have to keep in mind that these questions are very similar to the "assumption" questions, with one very important difference. If you remember from the previous articles, an assumption on the LSAT is an unstated premise that HAS TO BE TRUE in order for the conclusion to be true. In other words, if you need to check whether an answer choice is an assumption in an argument, you need to think of a scenario where that answer choice is false but the conclusion is still true. If you can think of such a scenario, then that answer choice is not correct. However, the exact opposite is true of the "logical conclusion" questions. **When checking whether an answer choice allows the argument's conclusion to be properly drawn, you need to think of a scenario in which the answer choice IS true, but the *conclusion* is not. Again, if you can come up with such a scenario, then that answer choice is not correct.**

EXAMPLE

> **Assad bought the newest digital camera on the market. As a result, Assad bought the most expensive camera in the store.**
>
> **The conclusion of the argument follows logically if which one of the following is assumed?**
>
> A) **Assad loves to buy expensive things.**
>
> B) **Cameras are among the most expensive personal tech items on the market.**
>
> C) **The newest digital camera is the most expensive camera.**

As with the previous question types, the first thing you need to do is to establish a clear picture of the structure of the argument, that is, what are the premises and what is the conclusion? You also need to pay more attention to the logical gaps, that is, are there any concepts that appear in the conclusion but not in the premises, and vice versa? For the simple argument above, the first sentence is the premise and the second sentence is the conclusion. Assad has the most expensive camera because he bought the newest digital camera.

As you can see, the premise is talking about how recently the camera was put on the market while the conclusion talks about the cost of the camera. Those are two different things, its release and its price. So that's the gap. The next step is to think of a sentence that closes that gap. The way you do that, in most cases, is simply by equating the new information in the conclusion with the relevant information in the premises. In this scenario we only have one premise and it's pretty obvious that all we need to do is equate the release with the price. Therefore, a potential bridge would say something like "new digital cameras are the most expensive". With that in mind, let's go through the answer choices.

Choice A is incorrect because it's not a statement that bridges the logical gap. This choice is tricky because it seems to be relevant and could potentially strengthen the argument. But remember, we're specifically looking for choices that bridge logical gaps, not just that strengthen the conclusion. Even if Assad loves to buy expensive things, that doesn't mean that he bought the most expensive camera. Maybe he bought the second most expensive camera, or maybe he spent all his money buying expensive clothes so that although he would've loved to buy an expensive camera he didn't have the money. **As you can see, we can think of a scenario where answer choice A is true but the conclusion is false, and so answer choice A isn't the one we're looking for.**

Choice B is also incorrect because it doesn't bridge the logical gap either and it's also tricky because it seems to be what the argument is talking about. However, it's not an assumption that's sufficient for the conclusion to be true. Even if cameras were the most expensive items on the personal tech market, Assad need not have bought the most expensive camera on the market. He bought the NEWEST one, which may have been less expensive than some used professional one that the store happened to have. The fact that other things are more or less expensive has no bearing on whether or not Assad bought the most expensive camera. In order to come to that conclusion you need information that relates that camera to other cameras, not other personal technology items.

Choice C is the correct choice because it connects the two concepts – new digital camera and most expensive camera. Since the choice equates the two, when we say that someone bought the newest digital camera we are also saying that they bought the most expensive camera on the market. And that's the way that these correct answer choices are going to function, they will allow you to make that move from the premises to the conclusion by making explicit the connection between them.

So the basic approach to doing these questions is to have a good grasp of the argument, and to look for the logical gaps between the premises and conclusion. There are a couple of variations to this question type, the most common is where instead of the gap being between premises and conclusion, it's between the premises themselves. So always keep in mind if there's a shift in the concepts whether in the premises or between the premises and conclusion. It's key to have a clear understanding what the premises and the conclusion are and what precisely they're talking about so that you can spot which answer choices are trying to trick you.

5.7 - Evaluate Questions

The 'evaluate' question type appears relatively rarely, generally less than once per LSAT. To evaluate an argument means to determine whether it's strong or weak; these questions essentially test your ability to separate relevant from irrelevant information. Common ways of asking the question are:

"Which one of the following would it be most helpful/relevant to know/investigate in evaluating the argument?", "The answer to which one of the following questions is most relevant to evaluating the conclusion drawn above?", etc.

This question is slightly different from the ones that have been explained up to this point because you're going to be focusing more on the answer choices; although knowing the structure of the argument is as important here as with any of the other questions the procedure for doing these questions emphasizes evaluating each of the choices in turn.

EXAMPLE

> **All of my tall friends have tall mothers. Therefore, children with tall mothers are probably going to grow up to be tall.**
>
> **Which one of the following would it be most helpful to know in evaluating the argument?**
>
> **A) Whether people who have tall fathers are also tall.**
>
> **B) How tall the author's friends are.**
>
> **C) Whether other people with tall mothers also tend to be tall.**

Ok, so as usual the first thing to do is to develop a clear picture of the argument, what are the premises and what's the conclusion. Here the first sentence is the premise and the second sentence is the conclusion, children with tall mothers are going to grow up to be tall because the author's tall friends all had tall mothers. Once you're done with that you need to be on the lookout for any shifts in meaning from the premises to the conclusion. Here the premise is about the author's friends, but the conclusion is about children in general. Can we conclude something about all people just based on the author's friends? Ok, so now we would move on to the answer choices and there's a specific procedure that we need to do with each choice. The choices are either going to be directly formulated as questions or (as here) they will easily be reformulated as questions. You need to provide two opposite answers for each question, and if one of the answers strengthens the argument and the other weakens it then that's the correct choice. If the answers are irrelevant, or they both weaken, or they both strengthen then that answer's not correct. So let's take a look at the choices.

Choice A is incorrect. If we reformulate it as a question we get "Are people who have tall fathers also tall?" One answer is "Yes, people who have tall fathers are also tall." And if we add that info to our argument we see that it's irrelevant. So now the author's tall friends all have tall mothers, and people with tall fathers are also tall. But that has no bearing on the conclusion because the conclusion is about children with tall mothers, it doesn't say anything about whether or not those children have tall fathers. And if we take the opposite answer to the question we get "No, people who have tall father's aren't tall." This likewise is irrelevant for the same reasons, neither the premise nor the conclusion have anything to do with fathers.

Choice B is incorrect. Phrasing it as a question we get "How tall are the author's tall friends?" One answer is "The author's friends are very tall." And we see that this answer is irrelevant to helping or hurting the argument because his friend's heights aren't what is supporting the conclusion, but the fact that they're tall. Likewise with the opposite answer "The author's friends aren't very tall." Maybe they're moderately tall, the point is that the author is basing his conclusion on what may be an unrepresentative sample, it's not his friend's heights that are the problem, it's that he's only using their heights.

Choice C is the correct answer. Phrasing it as a question we get "Do other people with tall mothers also tend to be tall?" One answer is "Yes, other people with tall mothers do tend to be tall." If that's the case then the author's argument is strengthened since his conclusion isn't based on an unrepresentative sample. The other answer is "No, other people with tall mothers don't tend to be tall." And this answer weakens the argument because it points out that the author is basing his conclusion on an unrepresentative sample. If other people with tall mothers aren't tall then the author can't conclude that those children in general will tend to be tall.

And that's the basic approach, for these questions it's key to have a clear understanding of what the argument is talking about and to carefully evaluate each answer choice, keeping in mind whether it's relevant or not.

5.8 - Principle (Justify) Questions

The "principle justify" question type appears regularly on every test. This question type is in essence a combination of strengthen and logical conclusion questions; you're being tested on your ability to pick the principle that makes the conclusion more likely by connecting the specific information in the premises to the conclusion. You can think of a principle as a general rule that is abstracted enough to apply to a range of situations and that lets you know how to evaluate a specific situation. Common ways of asking the question are:

"Which one of the following principles, if valid/established, most strongly supports the reasoning/argument/conclusion above?", "Which one of the following principles, if valid, most helps to justify the argument?", etc...

These questions test your ability to reason abstractly and identify general rules and categories. Let's take a look at this simplified example:

EXAMPLE

Maria-Cristina did all her homework and her chores. Therefore her parents should let her go to the movies with her friends.

Which one of the following principles, if valid, most strongly supports the conclusion above?

A) If someone is allowed to go to the movies then they did all their homework.
B) Parents should adopt a more permissive approach to raising their children.
C) Someone who fulfills their obligations should be allowed to do what they want.

Essentially, the argument will present you with premises that provide information about a specific situation, and a conclusion that is worded as a judgment, or more rarely, a prediction. The specific situation above is that Maria-Cristina did all her homework and her chores, while the judgment the author makes is that Maria-Cristina's parents ought to let her go to the movies. The correct principle helps you move from the situation to the judgment by providing a more abstract rule that can be applied to that situation. So, you first need to clearly establish the structure of the argument, then identify the main logical gap, and then think of the kind of principle that would help to close that gap. For example, we could address the above argument by saying "If Maria-Cristina did her homework and chores then she should be allowed to go to the movies." And that would bridge the gap and get us from the premises to the conclusion, or in other words, from the situation to the judgment.

Now, in order to make the statement "If Maria-Cristina did her homework and chores then she should be allowed to go to the movies" into a principle we would have to generalize it and make it about something more abstract. A principle wouldn't talk about Maria-Cristina and her chores and homework specifically, nor would it specifically talk about her being allowed to go to the movies with friends. Instead, it would have to use more general categories such as "people doing what they're required to do" as opposed to 'Maria-Cristina doing her homework and chores' and "people being rewarded" as opposed to "Maria-Cristina being allowed to go to the movies with friends." So the principle could look something like "If someone does what's required of them then they should be rewarded." And now we have a general rule that applies in Maria-Cristina's case.

The key thing to remember is that you should look for the gap and have a good idea of what's needed to bridge it but you also shouldn't spend too much time trying to figure out an exact principle because there might be lots of different principles that fit, depending on how abstract or specific the test-makers want to be. Instead, just have a general idea and go through the rules with that general idea in mind. Let's take a look at the choices.

Choice A is incorrect because although at first glance it seems like the appropriate general rule, it's actually got it backward. The choice says that people who go to the movies should have done all their homework. But the principle in our argument is the opposite; people who did all their homework and their chores should be allowed to go to the movies. Our argument says that Maria-Cristina did her homework and her chores and should therefore be allowed to go to the movies, not that Maria-Cristina is at the movies and therefore she did all her homework and her chores. **You will encounter these wrong answer choices with some frequency, where the principle is the reverse of what's needed, especially when you have principles that are stated as conditionals.**

Choice B is incorrect because it isn't relevant. This choice is tricky because it seems to be talking about what's in the argument; parents are mentioned and letting children do things are mentioned, but unfortunately, this choice also adds information that isn't found in the argument. Our argument doesn't say that parents should be more permissive; having a child do their work and their chores before being let out isn't an example of permissiveness. You can actually think of it as the opposite of permissiveness. The choice is appealing because on a superficial reading you may think of permission when you read permissiveness, in the sense that parents should give their children permission to do things. But that's not what the choice says or means, since permissiveness is defined as excessive freedom.

Choice C is the correct answer. We can restate it as "if someone fulfills their obligations then they should be allowed to do what they want," and now we can check to see if it matches up with the conclusion in the argument. "If someone fulfills their obligations" is a more general category that captures the premise in our argument – "Maria-Cristina did her homework and her chores", and "they should be allowed to do what they want" is likewise a more general category that captures the conclusion in our argument – "Maria-Cristina should be allowed to go to the movies with her friends." Therefore this principle works as a general rule that helps move the specific situation in the premises to the judgment in the conclusion.

And that's generally how these questions will work; for the most part the answer choice will be a conditional – or as in this case a statement that can easily be reformulated as a conditional – and you need to check to see if it's a more general rule that will help bridge the premises and conclusion. A common variation for the correct answer would be where instead of a straightforward conditional you'll get a contrapositive of the conditional that closes the gap. So in this case a correct answer would also have looked like "If someone didn't get what they wanted then they didn't fulfill their obligation." And another common variation on the correct choice is where it's not a conditional but is instead a more abstract statement that can actually be thought of as a principle behind the conditional principle that you may have come up with. So in this case that might look something like this: "It's important to have rewards for responsibility." These variations tend to be tricky because the correct choice doesn't correspond to what you may come up with initially and the categories it presents (importance of rewards, responsibility) tend to be abstract. The way to generally do these questions is to focus most of your emphasis on eliminating the wrong answers.

Ok, in addition to this kind of argument that we just went over you'll also encounter a variation where you actually won't be dealing with an argument at all but instead you'll be presented with a scenario and asked to find a corresponding generalization that fits with the info in the scenario. These questions appear more rarely and the approach is slightly different since you're not looking to close any logical gaps between premises and conclusion. But in essence you're still making more abstract categories of the specific info in the content. The important thing here is to look for the key concepts and generalize from them. So an example could be:

> **My daughter Maria-Cristina didn't do her chores or homework regularly until I started preventing her from going to the movies with her friends.**

So an acceptable generalization for this would focus on the key concepts of chores, homework, and preventing someone from going to the movies and might sound something like this: *children won't adopt responsible behavior unless their privileges are taken away.* So once again, the point is to locate the important concepts and use more abstract categories.

5.9 - Principle (Scenario) Questions

The 'principle scenario' question type appears regularly on just about every test and you can think of them as the reverse of the 'principle justify' question type. For the 'principle justify' question types you're evaluating an argument to identify the principle that it uses, for the 'principle scenario' types you're looking at a principle and identifying the argument that uses it. Common ways of asking the question are:

"Which one of the following most closely conforms to the principle above?", "Which one of the following conforms most closely to the principle illustrated by the argument above?", "Of the following, which one most closely conforms to the principle that the passage illustrates?", etc.

As with the previous question type these questions essentially test your ability to reason abstractly and identify specific instances/cases of general rules and categories. So basically you'll be dealing with one of three possibilities. In the content you'll either simply have a statement of a principle, or an argument that rests on a principle to provide justification for the conclusion, or a scenario that isn't an argument but that illustrates a general principle or rule. The most common variation is where you're simply presented with the principle.

EXAMPLE

If you go to church every day then you're religious.

Which one of the following most closely conforms to the principle above?

    A) Wojtech doesn't go to church every day therefore Wojtech isn't religious.

    B) Maseo goes to temple every day, therefore she's religious.

    C) Ludmila isn't religious therefore she doesn't go to church every day.

Ok, so in this case there's no argument or scenario just the principle and the first thing we need to do is to establish a clear picture of what it's saying. Most of the questions will be like this, although the principle itself will not necessarily be as straightforwardly presented as a conditional. Basically if you can you want to rephrase it as a conditional with clear sufficient and necessary conditions; in this case going to church every day is the sufficient condition and being religious is the necessary condition. The next step is to take this principle and go through the answer choices and see which one of the specific scenarios presented fits with the general rule in the principle.

Choice A is incorrect. A is tricky and it's an answer choice that's bound to come up in virtually every example of this question. It's incorrect because it's an example of a false negation. The conditional principle says that if you *go* to church then you *are* religious whereas choice A says that Wojtech *doesn't* go to church and therefore *isn't* religious. The sufficient and necessary conditions don't match up with the premise and the conclusion. If this choice were to say that Wojtech does go to church and therefore is religious then it would be correct. This will come up a lot so you need to be on the lookout for it. Likewise, you'll also often see examples of false reversals. For example, if the choice were to say that Wojtech is religious and therefore Wojtech goes to church every day that would also be incorrect because it switches the two conditions.

Choice B is incorrect because there's a subtle shift in the concepts used. The choice says that Maseo goes to *temple*, but the principle doesn't talk about *temple* it talks about *church*. The two concepts may be related but there's still a shift and you have to pay attention to exactly what the choice is saying. This is likewise something that you'll encounter fairly often, where the incorrect choice will look appealing but will have a subtle shift in a key concept.

Choice C is the correct choice; it doesn't seem to be an application of the general principle but in actuality it is, it's an application of the contrapositive of that principle. The principle is that if you go to church every day then you're religious, the contrapositive of that is that if you're not religious then you don't go to church every day. And the scenario in the choice is a specific example of that. Ludmila isn't religious – that's the premise and it matches with the sufficient condition in the contrapositive of the general principle, and she doesn't go to church every day – that's the conclusion and it matches with the necessary condition of the contrapositive of the general principle. The correct choices will have scenarios that directly present the general principle, but you will also have a lot of situations like this where the scenario presents the contrapositive of the general principle.

In addition to the variation that we presented above you'll also have situations where the content isn't a general principle but an argument where you have to figure out what the general principle is. In that case you need to follow the procedure that we outlined for 'principle justify' questions with the only difference being that the answer choice isn't the principle but another argument that uses it. These variations are less common. Likewise you'll also encounter variations where the content isn't an argument but a scenario and there you'll also have to do the same thing as for that kind of variation in the 'principle justify' question type.

The basic approach to doing these questions is to have a good grasp of the principle in the content and to pay attention to the answer choices so that you're not tricked by reversals in the conditions or shifts in meaning.

5.10 - Inference Questions

The 'inference' question type appears regularly on every test though they don't appear as often as 'strengthen/weaken' or 'assumption' questions. Here the content is generally not an argument and these questions test your ability to understand what exactly a piece of information allows you to conclude, deduce, or assume. Common ways of asking the question are:

"If the statements above are true, which one of the following must be true?", "The statements above, if true, most support which one of the following?", etc

An inference is something that is true because of other information that you have; you'll be asked to pick the answer choice that is going to be true just based on the information in the passage and not on anything else. This question type is very similar to the 'must be true' question type in the logic games section. The trick is basically to see if you can make an answer choice false; a choice that *can* be true isn't necessarily an inference, an inference *has* to be true.

EXAMPLE

> **All fishermen have good luck charms. Fisherman Jones is very skilled at catching tuna.**
>
> **If the statements above are true, which one of the following must be true?**
>
> **A) All fishermen that have the same good luck charms as Jones are skilled at catching tuna.**
>
> **B) Fisherman Jones is not as skilled at catching salmon as at catching tuna.**
>
> **C) Fisherman jones has a good luck charm.**

Basically, for these question types you're going to shift your emphasis to the answer choices, they're the most important thing to analyze. First, if there's an argument you need establish a clear picture of its structure; and if there's no argument you need to determine what the relationship is between the premises and what the key concepts are. Here we don't have an argument, and most of the inference questions actually won't have arguments, they'll be collections of statements. This one talks about fishermen, their good luck charms, and a specific fisherman and his abilities with a specific fish. Once we're done with that we need to go through the answer choices looking for the one that has to be true by eliminating the incorrect choices.

Remember, an inference has to be true. Essentially the incorrect choices will generally have new information, or there will be subtle shifts in terms, or it could be true but won't have to be true. The correct choices will also generally be either a synthesis of pieces of information from different sentences in the passage, or a restatement of a piece of information, or a consequence/necessary condition of information in the passage. That's what you need to be on the lookout for as you're going through the choices. And importantly, **something that has to be true can't be falsified so if you take the negative of an answer choice and it fits with the info in the passage then you know it's not an inference.** We call that the 'negation test' and you can use it when you're not sure about a choice. Ok, so let's take a look at the choices.

Choice A is incorrect, it could be true but there's no reason to think that it has to be true. If we say that not all the fishermen that have the same good luck charm are as good at catching tuna there's no conflict with our statements in the passage so we see that it's not an inference. Likewise you see that this is not a synthesis, restatement, or consequence of information in the passage.

Choice B is incorrect, it adds new information and since we don't have any basis to judge that information we can't say that it has to be true. The statements don't talk about salmon at all, so we can say that perhaps Jones is just as skilled at catching salmon as tuna and there wouldn't be any contradiction or conflict, so we see that it's not an inference. And once again, it's not a synthesis, restatement, or consequence.

Choice C is correct, it's a synthesis of information in the passage. The first sentence talks about all fishermen having good luck charms and the second lets us know that Jones is a fisherman. So therefore he has to have a good luck charm. There's no way that we could take the negative of this – that fisherman Jones doesn't have a good luck charm – and it not be in conflict with the statements, therefore it has to be true and it's our inference.

Ok, so that's the standard variation for these question types where the correct answer was a synthesis of different pieces of information in the statements. The first talked about a characteristic of all fishermen, the second talked about a specific fisherman, and the correct answer pointed out that the specific fisherman had to have that characteristic. Ok, let's go over this other variation that comes up quite a lot.

Recent computer programs allow people to have video conversations with one another. As technology advances we will have programs that will allow multiple people to have video conversations with one another with everyone hearing and seeing everyone else.

The statements above, if true, most support which one of the following?

A) Communications technology is the fastest growing technology on the market.

B) A video conversation is not the same as a normal conversation.

C) People can use computers to communicate with one another.

As with the previous example what we have here is not an argument, it's just a collection of statements. The first talks about what you can currently do with some programs and the second one talks about future advances in the abilities of programs.

Choice A is incorrect because it adds new info. The statements don't say anything about communications technology in general, nor about the market, nor about the rate of technology growth in the different sectors of the tech industry. So we could say that maybe communications technology isn't the fastest growing technology on the market and there would be no conflict with our statements, so the choice doesn't have to be true.

Choice B is incorrect because it could be true but there's nothing in the statements that talks about normal conversations. These choices are tricky because they state what we know to be plausible and likely but they aren't inferences, they aren't consequences of the information in the passage because there's nothing in the passage that, in this case, talks about normal conversations. Using the negation test we say that 'a video conversation is the same as a normal conversation' and there's no conflict with that so it's not an inference.

Choice C is correct because it's a consequence of a piece of information in the statements. The first sentence essentially says that people use computers to have video conversations with one another; and if that's true then that means that people use computers to communicate with one another since video conversations are a form of communication. If we were to use the negation test we'd say that 'people can't use computers to communicate with one another' but that is in direct conflict with our first sentence that says that there are programs for video conversations. So it has to be true and is therefore an inference.

So as you see this variation is different from the first because you're not relying on putting together two pieces of information for your inference but are instead looking at one piece of information – computers allow video conversation – and the inference is something that is true just by virtue of that one piece of information alone – that computers allow communication. This variation is related to another, less common, variation where the inference is merely a restatement. For restatements you're going to have choices that are much closer to the actual wording in the passage, for example 'Because of recent computer programs it's possible to have video conversations.' And in addition you're also going to come across questions that are EXCEPT questions where the incorrect choices are all inferences and the correct choice isn't. The important thing to note there is that the correct choice isn't necessarily something that can't be true, it's just something that doesn't have to be true. The basic approach is the same just reverse for the choices.

5.11 - Can't be True Questions

The 'can't be true' question type is relatively rare, it appears less than once per LSAT, and as with the inference questions you need to basically keep in mind what the passage is talking about and concentrate on evaluating the choices, looking for contradiction and conflict. It's important to keep in mind that the question is **not** an 'inference' EXCEPT question, rather it's analogous to the 'must be false' questions in the game section. The question has several different wording variations:

"If the statements in the passage are true, each of the following could be true EXCEPT", "If the statements above are true then which one of the following CANNOT be true/must be false?", etc

All of the incorrect choices can be true (they don't *have* to be true, they can be irrelevant) but the correct choice can't be true, it must be false. The passage is generally not an argument, and the key is to look for conflict; as long as the choice doesn't conflict with the information in the passage then it could be true and it's not correct.

EXAMPLE

> **In order to make tasty, flaky croissants you need to use real butter, not margarine. Pastries with real butter have too much fat for people on diets.**
>
> **If the statements in the passage are true, each of the following could be true EXCEPT:**
>
> **A) Some croissants made with real butter aren't flaky and tasty.**
>
> **B) People on diets can eat real butter as a spread on sandwiches.**
>
> **C) People on diets can eat tasty, flaky croissants.**

So as we mentioned and as was the case with the 'inference' question type the passage generally won't be an argument and you'll generally just need to read it carefully so that you have a good idea of what it's talking about. If there are conditionals it's a good idea to diagram them. In this case the first sentence talks about croissants needing real butter and the second sentence connects to it by saying that pastries with butter are bad for people on diets. So then we'll need to go through the answer choices to see if there's any conflict. Conflict means that you can't create a scenario where both the answer choice and the information in the passage are true at the same time. As with the 'inference' questions be on the lookout for combinations of statements and when looking at the choices pay attention to new information as well as information that *could* be false but doesn't *have to be.*

Choice A is incorrect because there's no conflict with the passage. The first sentence says that any croissant that's flaky and tasty has real butter. But that doesn't mean that any croissant that has real butter is going to be flaky and tasty. Maybe you also have to use the right dough, bake at the right temperature, etc. So if it doesn't have to be true that every croissant made with real butter is flaky and tasty then the choice – that some croissants made with real butter aren't flaky and tasty – can be true. No conflict so it's incorrect. This kind of choice is tricky because it doesn't add any info and at first glance it seems like there's conflict.

Choice B is incorrect because it adds new and irrelevant info. The passage says that *pastries* with real butter have too much fat for people on diets. It doesn't say that people on diets can't have any butter or that they can't have sandwiches with real butter. Maybe pastries use a lot more butter than sandwiches, maybe they have other things (sugar, etc) that compound the negative health effects for people on diets, maybe you can eat a lot more of them, etc. So it's certainly possible to have a scenario where the choice is true and there's no conflict with the passage.

Choice C is correct because it's in direct conflict with a synthesis of info from the passage. Tasty flaky croissants are a pastry that uses real butter and people on diets can't eat pastries with real butter. So the inference is that people on diets can't eat tasty, flaky croissants. And this is in direct conflict with the choice which says that they can. There's no scenario that can reconcile these two things so it can't be true.

And this was an example of the common variation for this question type where the correct choice was in conflict with a synthesis of the information in the passage. Another common variation is also analogous to the 'inference' type where instead of a synthesis the choice will be in conflict with a consequence of a single piece of info. For example if one of the choices was 'people on diets can eat any kind of pastry', this would be in conflict with the second sentence since pastries with real butter are a kind of pastry that people on diets can't eat. The basic approach is to have a good idea of what the passage is talking about and to go through the choices looking for new and irrelevant info and for things that can but don't have to be false and to keep in mind that the correct choice will be in conflict, generally with either a synthesis of the info in the passage or of a consequence/assumption of a piece of info.

5.12 - Formal Logic

Formal logic is a type of logic that you'll find in some of the arguments questions. The content in those questions will have a specific vocabulary and structure, and although these types of questions don't appear very often, to do them you need to use a specific approach.

EXAMPLE

All people are mammals, and some people are lawyers. No sharks are mammals. Therefore no lawyers are sharks.

What makes this example different from the ones that we've gone over previously is that these arguments involve qualifiers that relate two things, ideas, or concepts. The qualifiers, most of which were presented above, are: **all, most, some, some are not, most are not, and none.** Questions dealing with formal logic will require an understanding of these qualifiers.

All

"All A are B"

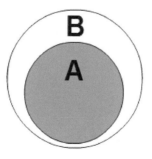

"All" means everyone or everything. For example, if we say that all dogs are animals we're saying that every element in the first group (dogs) is part of the second group (animals).

As you can see, this is our standard everyday meaning, where "all" means 100%. It is important to realize that "all" is not reversible, that is, "all dogs are animals" doesn't lead to "all animals are dogs". This is often tested on questions dealing with formal logic, so keep in mind that if a premise says "all A are B", you can't automatically assume that "all B are A."

In addition, we have to know the negative of each qualifier and the negative of "all" is "some are not". A common mistake here is to think that the negative of "all" is "none", but this is not the case. For example, "not all dogs are animals" means that "some dogs aren't animals," not "no dogs are animals". So let's take a closer look at that qualifier.

Some are not

"Some A are not B"

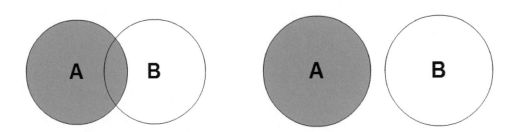

This qualifier is the negative of "all" and vice versa. The way that we represent these qualifiers is by having two circles that don't completely overlap, or that are completely separate (since remember 'some are not' could mean none or 0%), like in the diagram above.

For example, if we say that "some animals aren't pets" what that means is that there is at least one element in the first group (animals) that's not part of the second group (pets). Ie, the puff adder snake is an extremely dangerous animal that is not normally kept as a pet. However, if "all" means 100% then "some aren't" means anything less than 100%, including 0%. Now, this means that on the LSAT, "some aren't" is different from its everyday meaning because it includes 0%, or "none" and so our premise here could potentially mean that no animals are pets.

"Some are not" is not reversible either. In other words, saying that "some A aren't B" doesn't automatically imply that "some B aren't A". For example, if we say that "some mammals aren't doctors," that doesn't mean that the reverse is true and that "some doctors aren't mammals."

No

"No A are B"

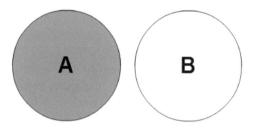

We've mentioned "none" a couple of times, which is generally expressed through "no". "No" means no one or nothing. For example, consider the statement "no dogs are cats". What that means is that no element in the first group (dogs) is part of the second group (cats). "No" has a standard everyday meaning, you can think of it as being 0%. And unlike most qualifiers, "no" is reversible – if no dogs are cats then we can automatically infer that no cats are dogs. The way that we represent this qualifier is by having two circles that don't have any overlapping area, as you see above.

In addition, the negative of "no" is "some", it's not 'all'. So to negate the premise "no dogs are cats", we would say: "some dogs are cats".

"Some A are B"

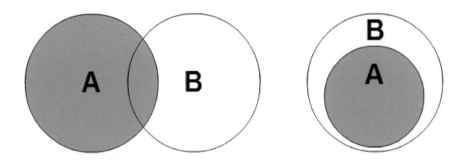

"Some" is the negative of "no". Let's take a look at this new premise: "some cats are independent". "Some" means anything above 0%, including 100%; there is at least one element in the first group (cats) that is part of the second group (independent things). This is slightly different from the everyday meaning of "some" because it includes "all". So our premise could be interpreted to mean that all cats are independent. Just like "no", "some" is reversible – if a premise says "some A are B" you can automatically assume that "some B are A". For example, if "some cats are independent" then we can automatically infer that "some independent things are cats". The way to represent this qualifier is to have the two circles overlap at some point, and remember that they could overlap completely with either one inside the other (remember "some" includes 100%).

"Most A are B"

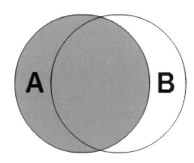 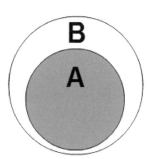

"Most" and "most are not" are slightly different from the qualifiers that we've gone over because they're technically not formal logic qualifiers but they appear often so we'll cover them as well. Let's take a look at this premise: "most paintings are art". "Most" means more than half, maybe all. More than half and maybe all of the elements in the first group (paintings) are part of the second group (art). Think of this as anything above 50%, including 100%. This definition is different from the everyday meaning because it includes "all", so therefore our premise could be interpreted to mean that all paintings are art.

This qualifier isn't reversible, meaning that if a premise says "most A are B", you can't automatically assume that "most B are A". Just because most paintings are art doesn't mean that most art is paintings. Plenty of sculptures, movies, music, and so on, can be considered art. The negative of "most" isn't "most aren't", it's "at most half". In the case of the statement "most paintings are art", the negative would be "at most half of paintings are art".

The way that we would diagram "most A are B" would be to have two circles where one of the circles is more inside the other than outside it. Since "most" includes 100%, a possible variation could be a diagram in which the first circle is completely inside the second.

Most are not

"Most A are not B"

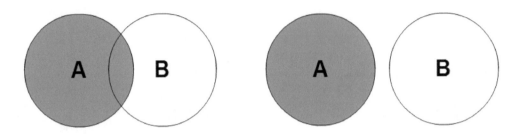

Take a look at this new premise: "most art isn't in museums". "Most aren't" means less than half, possibly none. So, this means that less than half – and maybe none – of the elements in the first group (art) are part of the second group (things in museums). This is different from the everyday meaning because it includes "none". This qualifier likewise isn't reversible, that is, if a premise says that "most A aren't B" that doesn't mean that "most B aren't A". For example, just because most art isn't in museums doesn't mean that most things in museums aren't art.

The negative of "most A aren't B" is "at least half". So, in the case of the statement "most art isn't in museums" the negative would be "at least half of all art is in museums." And the way that we would diagram this would be to have two circles where the overlapping area has to be smaller than the non-overlapping area on the first circle. Furthermore, since "most aren't" includes 0%, a variation could be a diagram in which the first circle is completely inside the second.

Combining statements with qualifiers

When you're presented with an argument that contains formal logic, what you essentially need to do is to diagram the statements using the venn diagrams I've shown you, and then to reuse circles for the elements that appear in more than one premise. Consider for example this set of premises:

"All A's are B's. No B's are C's."

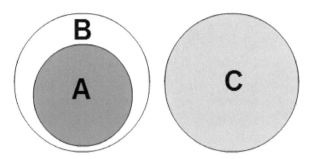

You would have the B's circle appear only once and that way you connect A's and C's. In this case we know that no A's are C's because the two circles don't overlap at all. However, just because it's in our diagram doesn't mean that it necessarily has to be true. In this case we're justified in concluding that no A's are C's but you need to remember that there are different ways of representing some of the qualifiers, and depending on which variation you choose you'll come up with different conclusions.

For example, take a look at this set of premises:

Some A's are B's. Some B's are C's.

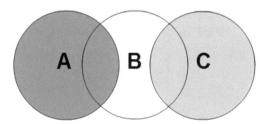 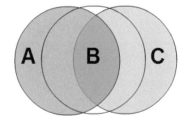

In the first diagram we have it so that A and C don't overlap and that's perfectly consistent with our statements. But in the second diagram we have them overlap, and that's consistent as well with our statements. So, we can't conclude that it's necessarily true that some A's are C's given the statements above. Therefore, you always need to pay attention to your diagrams and keep in mind whether there was some other way of representing them that would have given you a different conclusion.

5.13 - Formal Logic Questions

Formal logic questions are fairly rare and they aren't actually a separate type, they're questions that we've already gone over but the statements in the passage use the language of formal logic. They will sometimes be an argument and sometimes a collection of statements but they're generally recognizable through the use of the 'all, some, none, most, etc' qualifiers. And the questions themselves will be either 'logical conclusion' or 'inference' questions. These questions use the language of formal logic to test your ability to manage abstract information and the basic approach is to have a good grasp of diagraming and to know how to create diagrams to try and capture what you're looking for. Ok so let's take a look at this example:

> **No vampires are zombies and all walking dead are zombies. So no walking dead are shape-shifters.**
>
> **The conclusion above follows logically if which one of the following is assumed?**
>
> > **A) All shape-shifters are zombies.**
> >
> > **B) No vampires are walking dead.**
> >
> > **C) All shape-shifters are vampires.**

So this is a logical conclusion question variation and you're looking for the answer choice that provides information that makes the conclusion follow. Ok, so the first thing that you need to do once you see that it's a formal logic question is to diagram the premises. If it's a 'logical conclusion' variation then don't diagram the conclusion, leave it for the moment. And don't worry about using the 'correct' or 'best' diagram for the different qualifiers, just make sure to use the one that you're comfortable with. Ok so looking here we have two premises in the first sentence and the second sentence is the conclusion. The first premise is that no vampires are zombies and we would diagram that like this:

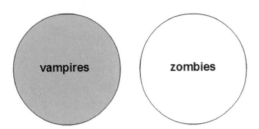

And the second premise, that all walking dead are zombies can be diagramed like this, where you add the circle for walking dead to the zombies circle:

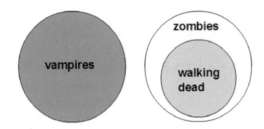

There are other ways we could've done that, with the two circles overlapping completely, but this is more intuitive and should be your first choice. Ok, once we've got this diagram we need to move on and incorporate the answer choices but try and keep them from making the conclusion true. The reason we do that is because there are conceivably different ways of diagraming a choice and not all of them will make the conclusion true; we're looking for the choice where whatever way you diagram it the conclusion will be true and so that choice has to make the conclusion follow logically.

Ok, so the first choice can be diagramed like this:

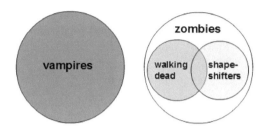

Drawing it like that we have a situation where there's some overlap between shape-shifters and walking dead so the conclusion doesn't hold. So we see that A isn't correct because we can draw it in such a way that the conclusion doesn't have to follow logically.

Choice B can be diagramed like this:

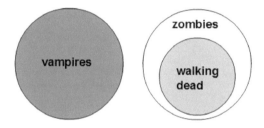

And that's actually just our original diagram so you see that the conclusion doesn't follow since we don't even have any information up there about shape-shifters. And that sometimes happens with the incorrect choices, where you're presented a premise that doesn't even connect the info in the conclusion.

Choice C can be diagramed like this:

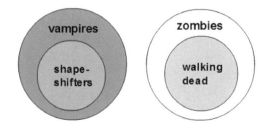

And looking at it we see that it represents the info in the conclusion, the walking dead and shape-shifter circles are completely separate, and actually there's no way that we can have this choice not lead to the conclusion because the two circles have to be separate since the vampire and zombie circles have to be separate and the shape-shifter circle has to be completely inside the vampire circle and the walking dead circle has to be completely inside the zombie circle. So this is the correct choice.

And this is the basic way that you need to do these questions. Just remember that with the 'logical conclusion' ones you're not diagraming the conclusion but are instead looking to see which of the choices makes it inevitable. Ok, now take a look at this example of the 'inference' variation:

All cats are furry. Some cats are wild. Some furry things are not striped.

If the above statements are true, then, on the basis of those statements, which one of the following must also be true?

> A) Some furry things are striped.
>
> B) Some cats are not wild.
>
> C) Some furry things are wild.

The initial approach is the same as with the 'logical conclusion' ones except that you'll diagram everything including any conclusion, although most of these passages won't have conclusions since they won't be arguments. So here we'll diagram the premises like this:

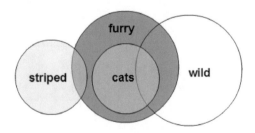

The important thing to notice here is that we simply drew these circles using the most intuitive way of representing them and we could've put together a different but equally valid diagram if we used other ways of representing the qualifiers. And in fact that's essentially what we'll be doing for this variation. In order to test if something must be true we see if we can falsify it and the way we do that for this question type is by using a different diagram that still means the same thing but doesn't represent the information in the choice. So let's take a look at the choices.

Looking at choice A we see that it's represented in the diagram, the furry circle and the striped circle overlap, and that's based on the last premise. But if we were to draw the last premise like this:

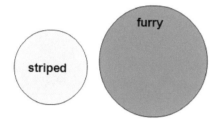

Then we'd get no overlap. And we can do that because remember 'some are not' can also mean 'none' and therefore just because some furry things are not striped that doesn't mean that some are. So choice A doesn't have to be true.

Looking at choice B, we see that it's likewise represented in the diagram, there are regions where the two circles don't overlap, and that's based on the second premise. But if we redraw the second premise like this:

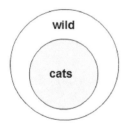

Then we see that the cat circle is completely inside the wild things circle and therefore it's not true that some cats are not wild. And we can do that because 'some' can mean 'all' and therefore just because some cats are wild that doesn't mean that some aren't. So choice B doesn't have to be true.

Looking at choice C, we see that it's likewise represented in the diagram, there's overlap between the furry things and wild things circles. And the reason for that is because the cats circle is completely inside the furry things circle and the wild things circle and the cats circle have to overlap because of the second premise. And there's no way of falsifying the choice because the wild things circle and the furry things circle have to overlap as long as the cats circle is inside the furry things circle. So that means that it has to be true.

This was the basic approach to doing these formal logic questions, the key is to be comfortable with diagraming and to pay attention to the different ways that you can diagram a premise.

5.14 - Paradox Questions

'Paradox' questions appear infrequently on the LSAT. These types of questions normally contain a passage that lays out two apparently contradictory pieces of information, or in other words, a paradox. Although these two pieces of information look like they can't both be true, they in fact can. Your job is to pick the answer choice that resolves the paradox by allowing both pieces of information to be true. The question has several different wording variations:

"Which one of the following, if true, does most to resolve/reconcile the apparent discrepancy/paradox/conflict in the information above?", etc...

Generally the two pieces of information seem contradictory because the reader tends to equate two things it is usually plausible to equate; the correct choice will cause you to notice and look critically at that equation. In order to do these questions you need to have a good grasp of the paradox and you need to carefully look to see what implicit assumptions you're making. Let's take a look at an example:

EXAMPLE

Industry reports show that less people went to the movies this year than last year. However, the film industry made more money this year than last year.

Which one of the following helps to resolve the apparent paradox?

> **A) Ticket sales are the industry's prime source of profits.**
>
> **B) Less movies were made this year than the previous year.**
>
> **C) The movie industry made record profits on DVD sales that more than compensated for lower ticket sales.**

Since the most important thing is to have a good idea of the paradox, you need to make sure that you identify it. Here the paradox is that less people went to the movies but the film industry made more money. Once you've identified this paradox, you need to evaluate it by trying to think of ways in which it's not really a paradox. Basically, look to identify what the differences are between the key elements in the two pieces of information and use that to get an idea of what kind of scenario might allow for all of the information to be true. But don't spend too much time because there are potentially an unlimited number of scenarios that could reconcile the seemingly contradictory info in the passage.

In this case we're dealing with a situation where less people went to the movies but the film industry made more money. Potential reconciliations are that maybe the price of tickets went up, or maybe the film industry got big tax breaks so they kept more of their revenue even if they didn't make as much as the year before. So with that in mind let's go to the choices.

Choice A is incorrect because it actually strengthens the paradox. If ticket sales are the industry's prime source of profits then it is definitely mysterious how it could've made more money as its prime source of profits went down.

Choice B is incorrect as well. The fact that less movies were made this year MAY explain why less people went to the movies, but it doesn't at all explain how it is possible that the film industry made more money at the same time. We are looking for an answer choice that explains how both could occur at the same time, which B doesn't do.

Choice C is the correct answer because it points out why an implicit equation between key concepts in the two pieces of information is invalid. Yes, less people went to the movies and this led to less profit from that revenue source, but more DVDs were sold and that increased the money coming in from another revenue source. Less ticket sales doesn't mean less money overall, it means less money from that source. Not only does this choice allow both pieces of info to be true, it is also an example of a choice that showed that an assumption that we were making (less money from tickets = less money in total) was unwarranted.

That is the basic approach to these questions. Remember to first identify the paradox, that is, figure out what are the two statements that are supposedly contradicting one another. Once you've identified the paradox, try to come up with a scenario that allows for both statements to be true. Finally, check the answer choices one by one. You're looking for a choice that explains how BOTH of the statements can be true **at the same time.**

5.15 - Disagreement Questions

'Disagreement' questions are generally two separate arguments in disagreement and they essentially test your ability to understand how an argument and a response are tied together. The basic approach is to have a good idea of what the argument are and how they're related, and then concentrate most of your energy on evaluating the choices. These questions appear regularly in every test and there are several different wording variations:

"The main issue in dispute between the two speakers is that ...?", "The arguments lend the most support for the claim that the two speakers disagree about the truth of which one of the following statements?", etc.

The passage will usually have two speakers, with the second speaker responding to what the first speaker is saying. The second speaker's argument may be directed against the first speaker's conclusion or support for the conclusion, or against an assumption behind the argument, or an implication of the argument, etc. You want to essentially try and figure out how the second speaker responds to the first and go through the answer choices looking for the one that the speakers respond to differently. Ok, so let's take a look at this example:

> **A: Roger Federer is the best tennis player ever. No one else has consistently dominated on as many surfaces.**
>
> **B: No, he was never dominant over Rafael Nadal. To be the best ever you need to establish clear superiority over your closest rival.**
>
> **A point at issue between A and B is whether**
>
> > **A) Roger Federer has dominated Rafael Nadal.**
> >
> > **B) Rafael Nadal is the best player ever.**
> >
> > **C) Roger Federer is the best tennis player ever.**

First, we need to determine the premises and conclusion of the two arguments. A says that Federer is the best because he consistently dominates on a lot of surfaces. B says that Federer never dominated Nadal because he never established clear superiority over Nadal. However, there's an implicit conclusion to B's argument and it's that

Federer's not the best because he didn't establish superiority over Nadal. Ok, now we need to determine the relationship between the two arguments. The second argument directly contradicts the first argument's conclusion. B is disagreeing with A's conclusion. What you in general need to do is determine how the second argument engages with the first, which part of the first argument is the second responding to and how? Once you're done with that you need to evaluate the choices by incorporating them into both arguments and seeing if there's conflict. If the two speakers have opposite opinions about the answer choice then that's the correct answer; if we don't know their opinion because it's new and irrelevant information or they have the same opinion then that's not the correct answer. So let's take a look at the answer choices.

Choice A is incorrect because it's not something that they have different opinions about. B certainly doesn't think that Federer has dominated Nadal, they say that explicitly. But we don't know A's opinion about that because A doesn't say that Federer has dominated any players, just that they've been dominant on the most surfaces. There are four surfaces in tennis and Federer has been dominant in three, Nadal has been dominant in the fourth. So since we don't know A's opinion of the point in choice A we can't say that they disagree.

Choice B is incorrect because it's also not something that they have different opinions about. A certainly doesn't agree with the choice, A thinks that Federer is the best player ever. But we don't know what B thinks, we just know that they don't think that Federer is the best player ever, but that doesn't mean that they think that Nadal is the best player ever. So once again, we don't have disagreement because we don't know the opinion of one of the speakers.

Choice C is the correct choice **because it's something that both speakers have different opinions about.** A agrees that Federer is the best player ever, that's A's explicit conclusion. B doesn't agree that Federer is the best player ever, that's B's implicit conclusion. So since there's disagreement that means that this is the correct choice.

And this is the basic approach and variation in these questions. You'll also encounter questions where the second speaker isn't going to directly attack the main conclusion in the first speaker's argument but instead a premise or a sub-conclusion.

5.16 - Method of Reasoning Questions

The method of reasoning questions appear regularly on every test and they ask you to determine what kind of reasoning the argument employs, so therefore the content of the passage will always be an argument. This question is different from the other question types that we went over in that here the question is about the logical structure of the argument. Whereas in previous questions having an idea of the logical structure was helpful only so far as it helped you answer what the question was here the question itself is about the logical structure of the argument, the answers will deal directly with the nature of that logical structure. The question has several different wording variations:

"Which one of the following most accurately describes the role played in the argument by the claim that ...?", "The claim that ... plays which one of the following roles in the argument?", "The argument does which of the following?", "Which one of the following most accurately describes the argument?", etc.

The basic approach to doing these questions is to have a good grasp of the argument, and to pay attention to the relationships between the statements. There are two basic variations for this question type. One question type will isolate a statement from the argument and ask you to identify the role of that statement. The other question type will ask you to characterize the nature of the argument as a whole. And the way that you approach the question will depend on which variation it is. In doing these questions it's more important to have a good grasp of the different sub-types for the question variations then it is to evaluate the answer choices so I'll present an overview of the different types of arguments that you're most likely to find as opposed to going over a couple of representative questions and answers as with the previous question types.

Ok, the first thing that you'll need to know is the overall approach to doing either major variation. The most important thing is to have a good idea of the relationships between the different statements in the argument. First, establish a clear picture of the argument, the subconclusions, and how many different arguments or points of view there are. Next, evaluate the relationships between the statements in the argument to see how they support the conclusion. Look to see if the statements reference one another in any ways: are they abstractions, examples, consequences, negations, etc. of one another. And also look to see if they perhaps form some sort of group, are they alternatives or conditions for something, etc. Then go through the answer choices looking for the answer that best matches what you've come up with.

Argument role

So for example here's a potential argument from the first variation, where you'll be asked what role a particular sentence/claim plays:

> **When a drug company develops a drug it makes a huge investment on the research. *Testing takes time and money.* Therefore it's justified for the company to get a patent on the drug.**

So a potential question might ask what role the italic statement plays. So looking at the overall relationships in the argument we see that the first sentence makes an assertion about what a drug company does when developing a drug. The next sentence provides an explanation/support for the first sentence. And the third sentence is the conclusion of the overall argument. Here the statement in question helps the argument, it provides support for a subconclusion – that drug companies make a huge investment – that in turn supports the overall conclusion. This particular argument is an example of one of the two broad types of statements for these 'role' questions. They help the argument. Other common ways in which a statement can help support a conclusion is by being a subconclusion, or by providing specific examples/illustrations that make the conclusion more likely. More generally, statements can add any kind of information or evidence that make a conclusion more likely. There are of course other ways in which statements can help an argument, but these are the most common. Let's take a look at this other common subtype of this first variation:

> **Pacifists say that one shouldn't engage in any violent acts. *But assume armed resistance was unavoidable.* Then the pacifists' philosophy seems less compelling.**

Here the first sentence presents a perspective or point of view. The second sentence presents a scenario that questions that point of view. And the third sentence is a conclusion that rejects the perspective from the first sentence. So once again, let's assume that this is a question where you're going to be asked what the role of the second sentence is, and in this case this is an example of the sub-type where the statement in question weakens an opposing argument. Statements can also function as weakeners, where they support the conclusion by raising some sort of consideration against another position presented in the argument. There are different ways in which that can be done, generally by bringing forward new information or evidence that in some way make the other position less likely, or by pointing out that there's conflict between the premises that support that position, or conflict between the premises and the position itself.

There are some other subtypes that you'll find for this variation, namely where the statements don't directly weaken or strengthen the argument, but in general most of the questions you'll find will be of this type. The basic thing to keep in mind with the answers to this variation is that correct answer is going to most accurately describe the role by correctly identifying it as a premise, claim, conclusion, subconclusion, principle, example, description, etc. and by correctly identifying its relationship to other statements in the argument. Incorrect answers will misidentify the statement or its relationship to the rest of the statements.

Argument as a whole

Ok, now let's turn to the other major variation in this question type, the questions where you'll be asked to characterize the nature of the argument as a whole. Take a look at this example:

> **Sam: This software company must make a lot more money than this law firm because they pay their starting employees more than twice as much on average.**
>
> **Susan: But you haven't taken into account that the law firm has a lot more employees and does a lot more business.**

Ok, so here we have two arguments. The first one argues that a software company makes more money because they pay their employees more. The second argument presents information that calls into question the first argument. This is an example of the major subtype for the second variation; questions where one argument references another. This is one of the two broad categories where the argument is structured so that the main argument that you're asked about references another argument. In this particular example the second argument directly attacked the reasoning of the opposing position. Susan points out an error in Sam's reasoning, he reasons that what's true of a part must be true of the whole. In addition to this example of the sub-type you'll also have situations where the opposing argument points out certain consequences of the position that it was criticizing in order to show that those consequences lead to undesirable conclusions. You'll also find arguments that show that there will be contradictions, that premises used to support a position might be used to argue against it as well, or it might use a slippery slope method.

The other broad category of subtypes for the second variation is arguments that don't reference any other argument in order to make a point. Just like the previous one this is also a broad category with several types of structures being represented. So for example let's take a look at a couple of different examples:

> **If a dog isn't properly housebroken before its first birthday then it'll never be properly housebroken. Fido hasn't been housebroken yet and he's a year and a half so that means that we won't be able to properly housebreak him.**

The first sentence introduces a general principle and the second sentence is a specific application of that principle. This is an example of a type of argument where the author reaches a conclusion simply by presenting information/evidence/examples, or principles. This is probably the broadest and most represented category.

> **Hawaii is an island in the middle of the Pacific Ocean and it has lush tropical vegetation, and Easter Island is in the middle of the Pacific Ocean so it must have lush tropical vegetation as well.**

Here the first part of the sentence is the premise, it tells us a couple of characteristics of Hawaii, and the second part is the conclusion, it concludes that Easter Island must share specific characteristics because it shares others with Hawaii. The argument draws an analogy between Hawaii and Easter island and that's the way that analogies work in these arguments, they point out that two things share something in common and that therefore they must share another thing in common.

> **I need to get dinner. Pizza makes me sick, lobster is too expensive, so I guess I'll grab a burger.**

The first sentence and the first part of the second sentence are the premises, the author has certain alternatives and needs to pick one. The conclusion picks one of the alternatives by ruling out the others. This is an example of a variation where alternatives play a central role. Another common variation is where the speaker presents something but then says that an alternative has an added advantage or doesn't have the same disadvantage.

For this question variation (characterizing the argument as a whole) the correct answer is going to most accurately characterize the overall structure by correctly identifying the basic components and fundamental relationships in the argument. The incorrect answers will use characterizations that aren't found in the argument.

The examples provided here aren't an exhaustive list but they should be useful to you to categorize and approach the different variations as you're doing them.

5.17 - Flaw in the Reasoning Questions

The 'flaw in the reasoning' questions are similar to the 'method of reasoning' questions in that here the logical structure of the argument is important, and just like those questions these 'flaw' questions appear regularly and frequently in every test (about five to seven per test, and they range from easy to difficult). These questions basically ask you to critically evaluate an argument and determine what's wrong with it. The flaw that you're looking for may be something that prevents the conclusion from being true, or simply an added consideration that would make the conclusion less likely. So that means that the content is always an argument, in order for the argument to have a flaw, there has to be an argument. There are several different wording variations:

"The argument is vulnerable to criticism on the grounds that it", "The reasoning is flawed because it", "A flaw in the reasoning of the argument is that", "The reasoning in the argument is questionable because it", etc.

There are a lot of ways of making a bad argument so there are going to be a lot of different flaw types. The basic approach is to determine what the structure of the argument is and how the premises support the conclusion. With that in mind, there are basic categories that the flaws fall into and in this article I'll present examples and common variations for them. Ok so let's take a look at some examples:

Causal reasoning

In last term's elections the conservative party mobilized its base and that's what caused them to win the majority of seats in parliament. This election cycle they didn't mobilize the base so they're not going to win a majority.

Ok so this is an example of **causal reasoning** and it appears often in the arguments section in general, along with being one of the basic categories of flaws for this question type. It's a causal reasoning question because the premise says that one thing caused another – the conservative party mobilizing its base caused them to win the majority of seats in parliament, and it concludes that the lack of that first thing is going to cause the lack of the second thing – them not mobilizing the base will cause them not to win a majority. In this specific case the flaw is that the conclusion rests on the assumption that nothing else will bring about the same effect; which isn't plausible in this scenario since maybe something else will cause the conservatives to win. Maybe because they're incumbents, maybe the electorate is satisfied with how they're running things, etc. In general whenever you see a 'flaw' question with causal reasoning where A causes B you need to think of four things to call into question the causal connection: **maybe it's just a correlation and not a causation, maybe something else caused B, maybe both A and B are caused by something else, and maybe B causes A instead of A causing B.**

This particular argument is an example where the conclusion is based on a causal connection in the premises; other variations are where the premises present information and on the basis of that the conclusion concludes that there's a causal connection. The flaw there is generally going to be one of the above four things. Also, you'll get variations where the conclusion concludes that a causal connection *doesn't* exist, A doesn't cause B because there's A without B and/or B without A, but the flaw is that the two don't always have to go together. So keep that in mind and be on the lookout for causal reasoning.

Justify

> **Michiko is planning on going to a restaurant in the neighborhood tonight. If she eats the chicken platter she'll have indigestion later, and if she eats the fish platter she won't be full. Therefore Michiko won't be satisfied when she comes back home.**

This is an example of the **justify** category. The structure of the argument is that the first two sentences are the premises and the third is the conclusion. Michiko won't be satisfied because if she eats one platter she'll have problems, and if she eats another she'll also have problems. But there's nothing in the argument that justifies the assumption that Michiko can only have fish or chicken for dinner. And that's the flaw, **the argument rests on a premise, assumption/implication of a premise, in order to get to the conclusion but this information needs to be justified.** Keep in mind that as you're going through the argument you should be on the lookout for premises that are open to dispute, the key is to see if there's anything unwarranted that needs to be justified. There are a couple of common variations for this type. One of the more common variations is where one of the premises is simply an assertion that needs to have something that gives you reason to accept it. Another one is where is something is argued against on the reasons that it leads to negative consequences. The unjustified assumption is that those negative consequences outweigh any positive consequences. And another common variation is where the conclusion rests on an unjustified generalization.

In addition to these examples the 'justify' category also frequently has questions where a key term in the argument is used in a questionable and non-standard way in the premises. The basic structure is that the premises will either explicitly or implicitly define a key term in a way that is open to dispute and use the term to come to a conclusion. The flaw is of course that the term is used in a way that is open to dispute without providing information that justifies why it's ok to use it that way. Another variation is where a key concept is defined in one way in the premises but then a conclusion is reached that's based on a different definition of the same concept. For the 'justify' category essentially you need to ask yourself – **are the sources of information questionable? Are the interpretations of ideas or events questionable? Is the framing of a situation questionable? Etc.**

Shift

> **You should get this phone because it's really cheap. It's almost $20 cheaper than the one with the camera, internet, and GPS.**

This is an example of the **shift** category. The structure of the argument is that the first part of the sentence is the conclusion, the second part is the subconclusion, and the second sentence supports the subconclusion. You should get this phone because it's cheap and it's cheap because it's cheaper than another phone. But just because the phone is cheaper than another, that doesn't mean it's cheap. What if the other phone costs $500, that way they're both expensive but the cheaper one is slightly less expensive. And that's the flaw, **the premises use a key concept in one sense but the conclusion uses it in another sense, it 'shifts' the meaning.** The basic structure will be that the premises will present information for one thing but the conclusion will be about something else, usually something subtly different so that it's not obvious that there's been a shift in terms. Here there's a subtle equation between something being cheaper than something else and it being cheap. There's some similarity with this category and some of the 'justify' ones in that you may also deal with assumptions and shifts in terms when looking at arguments where you need to justify something in the premises. But important difference is that those arguments are going to be far less subtle when it comes to problematic or questionable premises. Essentially you simply need to keep your eyes open and make sure that what the premises talk about is what the conclusion talks about.

Classical fallacies

> **Andee says we should legalize pot. But he's a dirty hippy so his argument is wrong.**

This is an example of what I call **classical fallacies**. They're argument **flaws that have a long history and are common in argument and rhetoric.** There are four of them that appear with some regularity on the LSAT. This is an example of the first one, and in this argument we have the first sentence as the premise and the second sentence as the conclusion. The author concludes that Andee's point is wrong because Andee's a hippy. But whether or not Andee's a hippy is irrelevant to his point. And that's the flaw, **arguing against someone by criticizing them and not the argument they're using to support their point is illegitimate and the classical name for it is** *ad hominem*. This argument type often appears with two speakers, though not necessarily. As you're going through the argument pay attention to the reasons that the speaker presents to undermine an opposing viewpoint, ad hominem arguments direct their attention to the source of the opposing viewpoint instead of the reasons supporting it.

> **Downloading music is wrong because it's against the law, and it's against the law because it's wrong.**

Here the first part is the conclusion and the second part is a subconclusion and the support for it. Downloading music is wrong and the reason that it's wrong is because it's against the law. That's a subconclusion and the support for that is that it's against the law because it's wrong. But that means that downloading music is wrong because it's wrong. And that's the flaw, **in order to conclude something you need to assume it. Another name for that is called** *circular reasoning*. The basic strategy for doing these correctly is to make sure that you have a good grasp of the argument structure and what the chain of reasoning leading to the conclusion is.

> **My grandpa fought in WW2 so his opinion on WW1 should be our guide.**

Here the first part is the premise and the second part is the conclusion. Grandpa's opinion on World War One should be our guide because he fought in World War Two. But just because grandpa fought in ww2 doesn't mean that what he thinks about ww1 is of any relevance. Maybe he doesn't have any direct experience with what happened in ww2 and hasn't informed himself about the history of ww1. And that's the flaw, **using grandpa as an authority for ww2 when there's no justifiable reason to do so is to commit the fallacy of *illegitimate appeal*.** Grandpa's authority is irrelevant or inappropriate to the issue at hand and so appealing to it is unjustified.

There are a couple of variations to this, one is where the argument makes an appeal to emotion – telling you to believe something because it makes you feel good. Pretty much all of advertising works like this. And the third common type is the appeal to opinion. Arguments that say that something is true because a lot of people believe it to be true are appeals to opinion. An opinion is by definition a belief that isn't supported by rigorous reasoning and therefore basing a conclusion on an opinion is incorrect. So those are the three basic variations that you'll get for the appeal flaws, remember pay attention to what it is that the argument calls on you to accept and determine whether or not it's warranted.

> **I've met a girl every time I went to this pub. So I'm definitely going to meet one tonight.**

Here the first sentence is the premise and the second sentence is the conclusion. I'm going to meet a girl because I've always met a girl. But just because I always met a girl before doesn't mean that I'll meet one tonight. That's the flaw, **using information from what happened in the past to conclude that the same thing will hold in the future is to commit the *future like past* fallacy.** The basic problem is that that's not necessarily a good enough reason. The basic thing is to look to see if the conclusion rests on assuming that what happened in the past will continue to happen in the future without added justification. Of course some events are always going to happen in the future – the sun will always rise, etc. – but the key is to see whether it is justified to assume that those events that will not necessarily always continue to happen are going to happen in the future. Ok, so those are the four major classical flaws that appear often on the LSAT so make sure to keep an eye out for them.

> **You say that if you know how to cook well then you went to a culinary institute. But Khan finished a prestigious culinary institute and doesn't know how to cook well at all. So you're wrong.**

This is an example of the **conditional** category of flaws. The first two sentences are the premises and the last sentence is the conclusion. If you want to know how to cook well then you went to cooking school. Khan did go to a cooking school but he doesn't know how to cook well. So it's not true that if you want to cook well you went to cooking school. But the first premise says that knowing how to cook well is the sufficient condition, the guarantee to going to a culinary institute. It's not a requirement for going to a culinary institute. Meaning that anyone you find who cooks well must have gone to a culinary institute but just because someone went to a culinary institute that doesn't mean that they cook well. So concluding that the conditional is false because the necessary condition is true and the sufficient is false is incorrect.

This particular instance is a common variation where a conditional is presented in the passage and then a conclusion is drawn based on a situation where the necessary condition is true and the sufficient condition is false. If it was the opposite where the conditions were mixed and the sufficient condition was true but the necessary false – for example if Khan knew how to cook well but hadn't gone to a culinary institute – then we could conclude that the conditional in the first premise is wrong. But that's the flaw here, that the conditions are reversed. This is a situation where the conclusion is about the conditional statement as a whole. Other common variations are where the conclusion is only about one of the conditions and this is where our common mistakes with conditional reasoning are usually found – the false negation and false reversal. So you'll have the conditional say 'if A then B' along with an additional premise that says 'notA' and the conclusion say 'therefore notB'. Or the additional premise might say 'B' and the conclusion will say 'therefore A'. Basically keep in mind **that the flaw is essentially going to be where one condition is interpreted to be the other and the conclusion is either going to be about the conditional as a whole or about one of the conditions.**

John's parents certainly went to the cinema tonight. They took their bikes and left in the direction of the park but tonight is Thursday night and they sometimes go to the cinema on Thursday nights.

This is an example of the **evidence** category of flaws. Here the first sentence is the conclusion and the second sentence is the premises. John's parents went to the cinema because even though they went in the direction of the park with their bikes they sometimes go to the movies on this night of the week. But even though there's some evidence that supports the conclusion, the conclusion asserts an unwarranted degree of certitude. The 'certainly' isn't warranted by the evidence since there's good reason to think that John's parents may not have gone to the cinema. And **that's the basic flaw, that there's some sort of problem with the evidence presented in the premises.** In this particular case, the premises present evidence that could lead us to conclude that John's parents went to the cinema but there's also reason to believe that they didn't and so the degree of certitude in the conclusion is unwarranted.

There are other variations, a common one is where the evidence presented is likewise consistent with the conclusion being true but in order for it to provide good support you'll need additional information. And another common variation is where the evidence presented is actually irrelevant to the conclusion. This example and the variations presented are one broad category for this flaw type, there's another broad category that's slightly different where the argument bases a conclusion on the fact that there's a lack of evidence. So just because something hasn't been shown to be dangerous we can conclude that it's safe. Or just because there's no evidence that the butler didn't do it, we can conclude that he did. For this category you need to keep in mind that if the premises say that there's an absence of evidence for something, then you can't conclude anything on the basis of that. So for this flaw you essentially need to pay attention to the information presented and think about anything that might be wrong with it.

Numerical

The book I just finished reading won more prestigious book awards last year than any other book published last year. Therefore it won the majority of the prestigious book awards.

This is an example of the **numerical** flaw type. The first sentence is the premise and the second sentence is the conclusion. The book won the majority of book awards because it won more of them than any other book. But just because it won more awards than any other doesn't mean it won the most. What if it won two awards and every other book won one out of a total of say ten awards. Then it wouldn't be true that the book won the majority. And **that's the flaw, we're talking about two different sets of values in the premises and conclusion.** The premises talk about the number of awards the book won compared to the number of awards that other books won, and the conclusion talks about the number of awards won compared to the total number of awards. The arguments that exhibit this flaw are similar to the 'shift' flaws because of the logical gap between the premises and conclusion but the concepts that you're going to be dealing with are going to be somehow related to numbers and amounts. In this case it was relative amounts of awards with the flaw being that the premise talked about the amount of awards relative to other books, and the conclusion talked about the amount of awards relative to the entire amount of awards. Essentially be on the lookout for that kind of shift between premises and conclusion where the premises talk about something in relative terms and the conclusion talks about something in absolute terms.

Sample

> **College students are all really good at math. My older brother's physics major roommates all know advanced math really well.**

This is an example of the **sample** flaw type. The first sentence is the conclusion and the second sentence is the premise. College students are good at math because author's brother's roommates are good at math. But just because the author's brother's roommates, who are all physics majors and are expected to be really good at math, know advanced math really well doesn't mean that all college students are really good at math. And **that's the flaw, the sample population that the author is using to base his conclusion on is not representative of the population that they're extrapolating to.** We can't say that all college students know math really well because the college students who are supposed to know it really well in fact do know it well. So, the basic structure is to use a sample to make a general conclusion, but the sample is not representative enough to warrant that general conclusion. When analyzing the argument look to see whether the evidence presents a sample group and carefully evaluate any ways in which the sample group might be different so as to place doubt on the conclusion that what is true of the sample group is going to be true in general.

Part/whole

> **The city is going to have to collect 100 tons of material to meet their quota for this year. But no borough is going to be able to collect that much recycled material. So the city is not going to meet their quota this year.**

This is an example of the **part/whole** flaw category. The first sentence is the premise and the second sentence is the conclusion. City's not going to meet the quota because no borough by itself is going to meet that quota. But just because no borough by itself is going to meet the quota that doesn't mean that all of them together won't meet the quota. I don't weigh 200 pounds but that doesn't mean that me and two of my friends together don't weigh 200 pounds. And **that's the flaw, it's not necessarily the case that what's true of each individual member is going to be true of the group.**

Another variation is where the premises conclude that a whole has a certain characteristic or quality and the conclusion then concludes that the parts have that characteristic or quality. For example the U.S. is wealthy and therefore everyone in the U.S. is wealthy. Another common variation is that something is shown to possess some characteristic that parts or members of some group possess and the conclusion is that this thing is also a part or member of that group. Essentially keep an eye out for arguments that have this division between a part or member on the one hand and a whole or group on the other. Just because something is true of one doesn't mean that it's going to be true of the other. And just because something has the characteristics or qualities of members of a particular group doesn't mean that it is a member of that group.

Two-person

> **John: According to a documentary I saw the other night, people who smoke regularly have a greatly increased risk of lung cancer, so you need to stop smoking.**
>
> **Jane: But that documentary only talked about people in their sixties. I'm only 45 so there's no reason for me to stop smoking.**

This is an example of the **two-person** flaws category. Ok, so the first thing to notice is that we have two speakers and two arguments an in fact this argument type is where two speakers are presenting their points of view, usually the second one is a response to the first, and usually the question asks for the flaw in the second argument. To do these questions we'll take a close look at both speakers' positions but we'll only evaluate the second one. John presents and argument where the first part of the sentence is the premise and the second is the conclusion. He says that Jane should stop smoking because people who smoke regularly have a greatly increased risk of lung cancer. Jane responds by disagreeing with him and her first and second sentences are the premises and the conclusion is implied. She doesn't have to stop smoking because John's source of information about lung cancer only talked about people in their sixties and she's 45. Although Jane has provided reasons that somewhat undermine John's argument, she words her conclusion as if though his point is completely false. There could still be plenty of good reasons for her to stop smoking. Maybe this particular documentary didn't talk about people in her age group but they're at risk as well, maybe people in her age group won't develop cancer but are at risk for other smoking-related diseases, etc. **That's the flaw here, the second person will conclude that the opposing position is false when all they've done is undermined it.** And that's one basic category that you'll find for these two-person arguments. The other common argument type that comes up is where the second person will simply not engage with the first person's argument and will instead disagree with or criticize a seemingly related but irrelevant point. The second person will simply miss the point. Ok, that's the two-person or two-position argument type. You'll always encounter two positions or arguments and in general the second position is going to be a person who presents a counter-argument to the first. The key is to make sure to look and see how it engages with the first.

Comparison

> **A country is like a company where we all work together for a common goal. So just like in a company where we let the smartest and most experienced make decisions, we shouldn't make policy decisions on the basis of what the majority wants.**

This is an example of the **comparison** flaw type. The first sentence and the first part of the second sentence are the premises and the second part of the second sentence is the conclusion. Majority shouldn't decide because a country is like a company and in a company we don't make decisions on the basis of what the majority wants. But just because a country and a company are alike in some respects, that we all work together for a common goal, that doesn't mean that they're alike in other respects. And **that's the flaw, there's a false comparison.** The argument presents two things and on the basis of that comparison there's a conclusion; however the comparison leaves out relevant information that would undermine the conclusion. Yes companies and countries are alike in some ways, but they're also different in other ways.

A common variation is where the argument compares two things to say that there's some sort of difference between them but doesn't include additional info that would weaken the conclusion. Great white sharks are bigger and stronger than pitbulls so they're more dangerous, but of course people come in contact with pitbulls much more often. The basic structure for this flaw category is a comparison between two things, either highlighting a difference and drawing a conclusion based on it, or equating them and drawing a conclusion on the basis of a purported similarity. Make sure to analyze the two things and to consider possible additional information that would undermine the conclusion.

Ok, so those are examples of the most common flaw categories that you'll encounter on the test. In addition to having a good grasp of the different kinds of flaws you're likely to find the most important thing is the ability to evaluate an argument and have a good grasp of what the premises and conclusion are and how exactly the argument is structured.

5.18 - Parallel Reasoning Questions

The 'parallel reasoning' questions are similar to the 'method of reasoning' questions in that you're dealing with argument structure, and they're similar to the 'flaw in the reasoning' questions in that many of the arguments that you'll be presented with are going to be flawed. So, the content is always going to be an argument and these questions appear regularly but not frequently in every test. They tend to be relatively more difficult because of their length since in essence you'll be dealing with six arguments. These questions basically ask you to replicate the structure of the argument in the passage and for the reasoning to be parallel the premises and the conclusion must match up between the passage and the correct choice. But the content of the argument doesn't have to be the same and the sequence of the statements doesn't have to be the same. There are several different wording variations:

"The reasoning in which of the following arguments is most similar to that in the argument above?", "In which one of the following is the pattern of reasoning most parallel to that in the argument above?", "The flawed pattern of reasoning in the argument above is most similar to that in which one of the following?", "Which one of the following arguments contains an error of reasoning that is also contained in the argument above?", etc.

For these questions the number and nature of the premises has to be the same, and they have to have the same relationship. The conclusion and the premises have to have the same relationship and the conclusion has to have the same scope and degree of probability. The validity or the flaw has to be the same (if the argument is flawed the question will always state that). There are a lot of different ways in which an argument can be structured so I'll provide you with some basic categories that appear commonly, just like I did with the 'flaw in the reasoning' questions. But the basic approach when doing these questions is to have a good idea of the different broad categories of types of reasoning, and to have a good idea of how the premises support the conclusion. First, establish a clear picture of what the premises are and what the conclusion is and then determine what the structure of the argument is by looking at the relationships between the statements as well as keeping in mind the different variations we're going to go over. And if it's a flawed argument determine the ways that it's flawed. Ok, so let's take a look at some examples.

Conditional

> If war is declared then we will either be invaded or we won't be invaded. If we're invaded we'll put troops on the border, and if we're not invaded we'll prepare an aerial attack. So if war is declared we'll either put troops on the border or prepare an aerial attack.

Ok, so this is an example of the **conditional** category of argument types. The first two sentences are the premises and the third sentence is the conclusion. The first premise presents a conditional statement where the necessary condition has two possible outcomes. The second premise is two additional conditionals where the necessary conditions from the first premise are used as sufficient conditions and additional necessary conditions are presented. So you're basically just linking conditions: if A then B or notB, if B then C, if notB then D – therefore if A then C or D. The conditional statement arguments are going to have premises that are conditional statements or just the sufficient or necessary conditions by themselves, and the conclusions follow from the premises. And most of those arguments are going to be worded so that it's obvious that you're dealing with conditionals. So for this particular argument the correct answer choice is going to be the one that has the same structure.

There are other variations, a common one is where not all of the premises are conditionals, for example there's a conditional with a couple of necessary conditions and one of them is ruled out, leaving just one necessary condition. Likewise you'll also find a broad group of conditional arguments where the conclusion isn't a conditional, and those arguments will all have the general structure where the conclusion is what must follow given the premises. And in addition to the valid conditional arguments it's a good idea to keep in mind some of the common ways in which conditional arguments are flawed. When it comes to the important basic elements, the valid and the flawed conditional arguments are more or less the same. But **there are a couple of errors that routinely appear and that we've actually covered in the previous articles – the false negation, and the false reversal**. So keep an eye out for those as you're going through the conditional arguments.

Quality/Characteristic

> Red apples are great for cider. These apples are yellow, so they won't be as tasty for cider.

This is an example of the **quality/characteristic** argument type. The first sentence and the first part of the second sentence are the premises, and the second part of the second sentence is the conclusion. Yellow apples aren't as tasty for cider as red apples because the red apples are great for cider. This category of arguments are going to deal with characteristics or qualities of groups or individuals and the relationships that arise between them. So as you're going through the argument try and be on the lookout for any situations where the argument identifies an individual or group as having a particular characteristic, as in this case that red apples are great for cider. And then pay attention to how that characterization and that actor relate to other actors in the argument and any other characterizations that come up. Like here that yellow apples aren't tasty for cider because they're not red apples. This is an example of a common, and flawed, variation where a group is presented as having a certain characteristic and then another group is concluded not to have that characteristic because it's not the same group.

Another common flawed variation is where things that have characteristic X have characteristic Y and therefore things that have characteristic Y have characteristic X. Valid argument types will be analogies where shared characteristics show that different actors are related, where a situation conforms in some fundamental respects to another situation. Ok, so these arguments deal with the characteristics or qualities of different things and draw conclusions based on their relationships. The important thing with this argument type is to pay attention to the different actors in the argument, how they're characterized, and how those characterizations are used to come to the conclusion.

Causality

> JuiceCorp. has achieved spectacular sales this year either because of its bold marketing campaign or because of new juices. But JuiceCorp had an even bolder marketing campaign last year but didn't have the same level of sales as this year so its sales are probably a result of its newer juices.

This is an example of the **causality** argument type. The first sentence and the first part of the second sentence are the premises and the second sentence is the conclusion. JuiceCorp's sales are a result of its newer juices because it's either a result of newer juices or bold marketing campaign and their marketing campaign was even bolder last year. Basically in this argument two things are presented as likely causes and one is ruled out so the other is determined to be the cause. As with the other categories for this question type we've gone over the basics for the 'flaw in the reasoning' question type and here we'll first focus on the valid argument types. If you're not told that the argument is flawed then you don't have to critically evaluate it using the tools that we developed in the previous sub-section for the arguments that involve causality; we just need to look to see if the premises, conclusion, and structure match up. In this particular example we concluded that one thing caused another because we ruled out another possible cause. This is a variation in the first broad category of causal arguments – where we conclude that one thing caused another.

Another variation is where the premises say that two things have been linked together in a lot of previous cases and therefore one causes the other. You'll also get variations where A doesn't directly cause C but instead causes B which in turn causes C. The other broad category is where we conclude that one thing didn't cause another. In these cases the premises point out that there's a correlation between two things but that correlation doesn't necessarily mean causation (it could be one of the things that we went over previously – maybe the cause and effect is reversed, maybe they're both caused by something else, etc) and the conclusion concludes that there's no causation. Ok, so the important thing is to pay attention to see in what way causal reasoning is used, whether the argument is making a claim that something *is* causally related to something else, that something *isn't* causally related to something else, or whether the argument is flawed and employs one of the standard errors of causal reasoning.

Numerical

The market share of laptops increased more than the market share of desktops from last year to this year. Therefore more people own laptops than desktops.

This is an example of the **numerical** argument type. The first sentence is the premise and the second sentence is the conclusion. More people own laptops than desktops because the market share of laptops increased more than the market share of desktops. Basically, these arguments are going to make a point that will require some sort of numerical reasoning – in general increase or decrease. In this case the argument is flawed because it talks about an increase in quantity in the premises, which is a relative change, but talks about an absolute amount in the conclusion. Maybe laptops had 5 percent of the market last year and they increased their market share to 10 percent, which is a hundred percent increase. And desktops went from having 95 percent of the market to 90 percent. So they decreased their share when laptops increased it, but does that mean that there are more laptops? No, there are still more desktops. The questions for this category are generally flawed arguments and this is a particular example of that.

Another variation is where an increase in X means an increase in Y and therefore an increase in Y means an increase in X. This isn't necessarily true, for example as a city's population increases that means that pollution increases but that doesn't mean that if pollution increases that means that the population increased. Maybe more polluting industries moved to the town. And another flawed variation is where the premises introduce statistics and probability but the conclusion isn't warranted. For example: 'the weatherman says there's a 90% chance of rain but there's no rain yet so it won't rain today'. So when doing these questions pay attention to how the concepts of increase, decrease, and relative vs absolute values are used, along with percents and probability.

Shift

> **John intentionally gave his girlfriend a chocolate cake because it was her birthday. But they didn't know she was allergic to chocolate and she ended up in the emergency room. So John intended to make his girlfriend sick.**

This is an example of the **shift** category. The first two sentences are the premises and the last sentence is the conclusion. John intended to make his girlfriend sick because he gave her a cake that made her sick. The flaw is that the word 'intentionally' is used in a couple of different ways, it shifts from premise to conclusion. In the premises it's used to show that John wanted to give his girlfriend a cake, and in the conclusion it's used to conclude that he wanted to make her sick. But he didn't know that she was allergic so he couldn't have given it to her with the intent to make her sick. And that's the basic structure of these arguments, as we went over in the previous articles arguments where there are shifts in terms what you need to make sure is to pay attention to what exactly the premises are talking about and what the conclusion is talking about and if there's any disconnect between the two.

Ok, so as you saw, the important thing here is to have a good idea of what the argument is in the passage, what the premises and the conclusion are, and to have an idea of how the reasoning is structured. You do that by paying attention to the relationship between the statements. And then you have to repeat that process with each answer choice where it is above all crucial that you have a good idea of what the premises are and what the conclusion is. The point is to make sure that the reasoning structure is the same in the two arguments and as you look at each answer choice you should try and come up with a summary of the reasoning in the answer choice to compare it to the reasoning in the passage; as well you will need to pay attention to the premises in both arguments – to see if you have the same number of premises, the same kinds of premises, etc, and you will need to pay attention to the conclusion – to see if it's the same kind of conclusion, and the validity. And as I've repeatedly mentioned, you shouldn't look at all of these things separately and sequentially, instead it's going to depend on the specific instance and of course in a lot of situations the reasoning structure is going to be different precisely because the premises or the conclusion is different.

Conclusion

We've just covered the different arguments question types that you'll encounter on the test and the way that you should approach them. The examples given were simplified versions of what's on the test and are designed to teach you the essence of each question type and the approach to doing them. The videos on my website provide an in-depth analysis for each variation of the different question types along with a detailed step-by-step approach to doing them. There are literally hundreds of actual LSAT questions that are explained on video and in the interactive exercises. If you're looking for tutoring, I structure my lessons around groups of question types where I go over specific questions with my students and I provide free e-mail explanations (be it for specific questions, or concepts that they may not understand) in between classes. Please check out my site lsat.totaltestprep.net for more information.

6

Reading Comprehension

Every LSAT is going to have one reading comprehension section (two if one of them is the experimental, unscored one). And this is basically the same reading passages that we've been seeing since grade school, of course the difference being that these passages are going to be denser and more difficult. There will be about four passages of about 400 – 500 words in length and one of them will be a double passage. It will consist of two shorter, related passages. The passages will be followed by 5 – 8 questions that test your understanding of the passage(s). The point of this section is to test your ability to read and comprehend dense material. Lawyers and law students need to be able to consume large amounts of information and to have a good idea of what they've read.

The passages generally deal with a topic in history, humanities/literature, the law, and science. The specific content of the passage is not important since the questions will deal with your understanding of the structure and arguments in the passage and not the details. The test doesn't assume that you have any previous knowledge or any in-depth knowledge of the topic. The information in the passage is simply a vehicle for the test to evaluate your ability to read carefully and understand dense material. The important thing to pay attention to in the passage is the structure and the reasoning, not the narrative or the aesthetic. You're not evaluating how well it's written or how artistically it's written. You're mainly paying attention to the point that the author is trying to make and the arguments and structure of reasoning that the author uses to make that point.

This section is difficult primarily because you're going to be dealing with dense reading passages and learning how to critically evaluate those is not just a question of learning the right approach but you also need to develop concentration abilities and mental stamina. And that isn't something that's learned like algebra or history but you actually have to spend a significant time practicing. That being said, there is a right way and wrong way of analyzing the reading passages and these articles will outline it for you.

And in addition, if you don't have a solid grasp of arguments and the logic and reasoning behind them you should go over those articles first because reading comprehension builds heavily on what you learn when you learn to do the arguments. You can think of the passages as a set of interconnected arguments, and the questions are going to be roughly similar to the questions in the arguments section.

6.1 - P.O.T.S. Introduction

As an overall approach to doing the passages you need to read critically. Practice developing a rich visual and conceptual structure as you're reading and not just sounding out the words in your head. Pay attention to the relationships between the sentences amongst themselves and their relationship to the passage as a whole. Understanding arguments is critical, if you need to, review the argument structure article. In order to have a good understanding of the passage that will allow you to best answer the questions there are four key things that you need to focus on as you're reading the passage:

- **P**erspectives: each passage is going to present the points of views or perspectives of anywhere from two or more groups or individuals, including the author of the passage, concerning the topic of the passage

- **O**ppositions/conflict: the perspectives of the different groups will generally be in conflict or in opposition, they'll have different evaluations and attitudes toward the subject in question

- **T**one: the different groups will present their perspectives in language that conveys emotions

- **S**tructure: The passage can be understood as an extended argument with the author's main point acting as the conclusion and the perspectives, oppositions, and tone all act together to manifest the structure of this argument

In addition to the things mentioned above you also need to keep in mind that the passages will generally have a certain amount of information that is presented, usually at the very beginning, that acts as background or context for the rest of the passage.

6.2 - Perspectives

In order to have a good understanding of the the passages you will encounter on the reading comprehension portion of your LSAT, as you're reading the passage you will need to focus on four key elements: perspectives, oppositions, tone, and structure. Here we'll take a look at perspectives, while the next three sub-sections will deal with oppositions, tone, and structure, respectively.

Each passage contains a series of arguments, and the very beginning of each passage will generally provide you with context for the arguments in the rest of the passage. The basic organizing principle for every reading passage is that the author will present multiple perspectives concerning the subject of the passage. For example, a passage may be about education policy in the United States, and in that case, the perspectives of educators, politicians, and students may be present in the passage.

Putting multiple perspectives in a passage makes sense since the actual practice of the law is based on a judge evaluating between contending perspectives in a court room, or jurors evaluating contending perspectives from witnesses, or several lawyers representing the contending interests of their clients in a negotiation, etc. However, remember that not every perspective will have equal representation. Since the author's perspective is always one of the contending perspectives and is the one that ties everything together, he or she might be more sympathetic to one perspective rather than another.

In the passage

Perspectives are generally found at the beginning of the passage, within the first two paragraphs, and they establish the main fault lines of the argument. However, they could also be found throughout the entire passage as the main characters refine and elaborate their positions.

The first basic variation is where the author presents the views of a certain group and then says that there's something wrong with that position. This generally happens in the beginning of the passage, with the views of the group coming first and the author's perspective at the very end of the first paragraph or at the beginning of the second. For example, the author may say that professors of creative writing at most universities believe that poetry and fiction should be taught separately, although this belief enforces a false distinction between the two genres. Then, throughout the rest of the passage, positions that are established at the beginning of the passage are further elaborated on.

The second basic variation is one in which the author presents several perspectives concerning a topic but doesn't directly challenge any of them. The number of perspectives starts at two but can easily be three, four, five, or more. The perspectives can be further grouped together into larger blocs and contrasted with one another. The author may ultimately most closely identify with one perspective or he or she may simply draw a conclusion that in some way incorporates an analysis of all of the different perspectives.

As you're reading

Pay attention to sentences that introduce groups or individuals. "Legal scholars specializing in international law have maintained that ...", "The consensus among literary critics has been ...", "With recent advances in technology marine biologists have begun to change their opinions concerning ...", "Mark Twain always considered his early pieces of journalism ...", etc. Note their perspective and the reasoning that is used to support that perspective and note the relationship between the different perspectives. In general the relationship will be one of opposition so look for the points of conflict.

Pay attention to the author's voice. Since the author's perspective won't be as obviously articulated, you need to learn to differentiate between those sentences in which the author presents his or her perspective and those sentences in which he or she evaluates someone else's perspective. Furthermore, it's often helpful to diagram. For example, you could circle the words that identify the group whose perspective is being presented, and then underline the basic point advanced by that group.

Perspectives are a key element in any reading comprehension passage and they provide the backbone for the overall development of the passage. An ability to spot perspectives will help you develop a mental map of the overall passage. We've been talking about contending or conflicting perspectives from different groups. This implies that there is an opposition between the positions that the different groups take, and that's another central element to our analysis of the passages, one which we'll move on to now.

6.3 - Oppositions

Each passage will have multiple contending perspectives and the fact that they're contending means that they're in opposition; this just means that the speakers disagree. For example, a certain passage may contrast the claims of owners of intellectual property (authors, musicians, artists, etc...) with the claims of everyday internet users. The owners of intellectual property may feel that intellectual property on the internet is not protected well enough, while the everyday internet user may feel that access to information on the internet is getting reduced at a greater and greater pace. Such oppositions are tremendously important in the reading passages because they're an important structural element in how the overall argument is laid out. The basic opposition is between the major perspectives, but oppositions also appear within the arguments and within the expositions that develop the major perspectives.

In the passage

The basic opposition in any reading passage is between the major perspectives (such as between owners of intellectual property and the everyday internet user). Since the perspectives are the points of view of different groups (including those of the author) on a particular subject, that conflict or opposition that is generated by the different perspectives provides the basic framework for the overall passage. As you read the passage and keep a mental summary of the development of the overall argument in your head, knowing that basic opposition makes it easier to keep track of everything.

Oppositions are also found as the basic perspectives are developed and extended. As the basic perspectives are elaborated in the body of the passage they are further set in contrast to one another, highlighting their opposition to one another at levels of more detail. The arguments that are used to support major subsidiary points are often structured so as to show why a certain thing differs from something else – once again pointing out an opposition. As well, the author will often evaluate a group of perspectives or points of view by highlighting their difference.

As you're reading

Pay attention to sentences that introduce opposition and conflict. Look for words that signal disjunctive premises: **"however", "but", "although", "on the other hand"**, etc. Note when the perspective shifts and whether or not the perspectives are in opposition. Pay attention to the relationships of a sentence to the sentences around it. It's helpful to diagram; for example you could bracket the words that signal disjunction. In general, as you get better at spotting the oppositions in a passage, you will get better at keeping track of the overall argument of what you read, which will in turn help you understand the reading comprehension passages better.

6.4 - Tone

The author of the passage is not neutral about what he or she is presenting. Almost always, the author will have an opinion and attitude towards the different perspectives and arguments laid out in the passage, and that attitude, or tone, is conveyed in the author's choice of words. Words that reveal the state of mind of the speaker are words that convey tone. The other individuals or groups whose perspectives are presented in the passage will also present their information with an emotional overlay, but, you have to keep in mind that their positions are presented via the author so their actual attitude may be unclear. For example, the author may SAY that modern neuroscientists look down on the attempts of evolutionary biologists to try to explain in a Darwinian fashion the origin of music. However, whether or not modern neuroscientists actually look down on anyone is not so clear.

In the passage

Broadly speaking, the author will either be sympathetic/positive or unsympathetic/negative towards the different perspectives. The author's tone will however, often be more complex, and will often convey more than simple support or disagreement. The author's tone will be presented throughout the passage as the overall argument is developed.

As you're reading

Pay attention to words that convey emotion. The author may articulate his or her tone while introducing a perspective or while developing one. In general, it's a good idea to be aware of tone because several questions in the reading comprehension section hinge on being able to spot tone. As well, understanding the author's tone can be helpful in keeping track of the oppositions in the overall argument in the passage.

6.5 - Structure

Each reading passage is an extended argument. The author has a main point that he or she is looking to communicate and that point is supported throughout the passage. The passage elements that we went over – perspectives, oppositions, tone – are important in determining the overall structure of the extended argument in the passage. It's necessary to have a good understanding of the logic of the arguments in order to understand the relationships within the passage.

In the passage

Generally, the first paragraph presents the fundamental conflict along with background context while the rest of the paragraphs develop the overall argument, and the last paragraph offers a summation or articulation of the main point. A common variation is to have the passage introduce a perspective and the author present a counter to that perspective – either his or her own or one that the author supports; the rest of the paragraphs in the passage will generally elaborate on the author's perspective and identify the points of conflict. Another common variation is to have the passage introduce several contending perspectives in the first paragraph without the author identifying with one; the rest of the paragraphs will then generally elaborate on the different perspectives and their points of conflict more equally and at some point present the author's analysis. The main point may be explicitly present in the passage, either in the first paragraph or the last. The main point is the summation of the information in the passage from the author's perspective.

As you're reading

The most important thing is to have a good understanding of the way the information in the passage is inter-related. Understanding the structure means knowing how the paragraphs are related to one another and how the sentences within the paragraphs are related to one another and to other sentences in the passage. The previous elements that we went over are all key to developing a clear picture of the structure. The backbone and basic relationship in any passage is between opposing perspectives. Oppositions aren't only found between perspectives but in the arguments that elaborate and detail the individual perspectives. Also, you need to look for perspectives, oppositions, and tone in each paragraph and as you're reading look for arguments and determine the premises and conclusion as well as background context. Once you're done with a paragraph make a quick one-sentence summary in your head to help you keep track of what you're reading. At the end of the passage, come up with a main point based on your analysis of the passage.

6.6 - Dual Passages

The dual passages are in essence the same as the single passages, they still test your reading comprehension though there is obviously more of an emphasis on comparison and contrast. The two passages generally aren't in direct conflict, they're not an argument and a response. You're looking to see how the passages are alike, how they're different, where they're in opposition, and where they're in agreement.

In the passage

Each passage is written from a certain perspective; each passage may or may not incorporate conflicting perspectives and the perspectives in the two passages may or may not be in direct opposition. The length of the passages taken together is roughly equal to a regular passage. In other respects the passages are basically the same as regular passages; content is drawn from the same sources as regular passages, etc.

As you're reading

Follow the same procedure as for the regular passages. Once you're done evaluating the passages individually, evaluate their relationship to one another

- In what ways do they approach their shared subject similarly?

- In what ways do they approach their shared subject differently?

- What do they agree on?

- What do they disagree on?

6.7 - Questions Introduction

The nature of the questions will be familiar from the arguments section. The reading comprehension tests your ability to evaluate and analyze structure/arguments. The majority of the question types will be ones you've seen before in the arguments section and the information needed to answer questions will always be found in the passage. You're not tested on what you know but what you understand. The questions won't require you to have additional knowledge of the topic in the passage and they range from specific to general. Questions that are more specific will require you to concentrate on a narrow area of the passage for the answer; questions that are more general will require you to analyze the passage more broadly and look at several different areas for the answer.

Dual passage questions are slightly different but broadly similar. A minority of the questions that you'll encounter will deal with only one passage and can be any of the types that you'll find for single passages. Most of the questions for double passages ask you to in some way analyze the two passages together by comparing and contrasting.

Question types

single passage

- main point
- author's attitude
- primary purpose
- inference
- direct information
- method of reasoning
- word definition

- principle
- strengthen/weaken

double passage

- (any of the single passage ones)
- coherence
- conflict
- irrelevance
- relationship

6.8 - Main Point Questions

Basic info

'Which one of the following most accurately summarizes/states/expresses the main point of the passage?'

Main point questions appear in virtually every passage as the first question after the text. The questions aren't difficult but not simple either, these questions are by definition general. The main point questions test your ability to identify and analyze the overall structure of the argument in the text; the passage is basically an extended argument and you're being asked to provide the conclusion. This question type is roughly similar to the conclusion questions in the arguments section with the obvious difference being scope. Conclusion questions dealt with a single argument and the relationships between the premises leading to the conclusion but main point question deal with all of the arguments and paragraphs in the passage and the relationship of their conclusions and summaries leading to the main point

Approach

Having a good understanding of the overall argument and being able to evaluate the answer choices is key. The first step is to have a prepared main point from your analysis of the passage. You don't have to write it down anywhere but you will come up with the main point once you're done reading the entire passage and these questions are almost always the first question and if not then the second. Next, evaluate the answer choices to see if they capture the correct overall main point. Analyze the choices to see if they focus on the correct scope by evaluating the concepts the choices use and whether they're too narrow, introduce new information, or mismatch the info from the text

Right answer/wrong answer

The correct answer choice will summarize the information in the passage. The passages are arguments and they're structured to lead to a particular conclusion, the correct answer will articulate that conclusion. The incorrect answer will not provide an adequate summary of the passage. The choice may be too narrow and only incorporate information from part of the passage, or it may be over-reaching in that it will conclude something that isn't supported by the text. Also the choice may incorrectly represent information from the passage and it may add new and irrelevant information.

Summary

Basic approach is to have a main point prepared and use it to evaluate the answer choices along with looking for the choice that adequately summarizes the information in the passage.

6.9 - Author's Attitude Questions

Basic info

'The author's attitude toward Roger Abraham's book can best be described as one of', 'Which one of the following can most accurately be used to describe the author's attitude toward critics of the Hippocratic oath?', 'Which one of the following most accurately identifies the attitude shown by the author in the passage toward talk-story?'

The questions generally include the words 'author's attitude', they don't appear frequently but you will find them once in every two passages or so. They tend to be a bit more difficult because the answers require interpretation, and range from specific to general but tend to be a bit more general. The author's attitude questions basically ask you to identify how the author feels about something in the text; you're being tested on your ability to pick up on the author's tone.

These questions are in the same broad category as the main point questions and the primary purpose questions in that you're being asked to analyze the author's perspective. They're a bit narrower in scope because you're focusing on what the author feels.

Approach

The most important thing is to have a good idea of the author's tone. First, you need to determine what the question is asking about and where you can find out what the author thinks about it. The object of the author's attention is relatively easy to find, but you'll have to make a bit more of an effort identifying where to analyze the author's language to see what they think about it. Then, you need to come up with what the author's attitude may potentially be; look at the author's word choice as well as the author's attitude towards other, related objects in the text. Finally, evaluate the answer choices against your potential answer and see if the choice accurately reflects what's in the text. The answer choices will generally be of the form of a qualifier and an emotion/attitude, ie: overwhelmingly angry, subtly condescending, etc. Both the qualifier and the emotion have to have support in the text.

Right answer/wrong answer

The correct answer will present a qualifier and emotion that are both supported by the text; the qualifier will not be too extreme and the emotion/attitude will be reflected in the author's word choice. The incorrect answers will not be supported by the text; the qualifier may be too extreme or irrelevant and not supported by the text and the emotion/attitude will not be reflected in the author's word choice.

Summary

Basically, make sure to pay attention to the author's language and have an idea of what their attitude is and then use that to evaluate the answer choices.

6.10 - Primary Purpose Questions

Basic info

'The author's primary purpose in writing the passage is to', 'The primary purpose of the passage is to', etc

Questions will ask for primary or overall/general purpose/concern of passage, not just purpose of specific part. These questions are relatively frequent, appear at least once every couple of passages. Primary purpose questions tend to be a bit more difficult than some of the others because the answer choices aren't directly stated in the text. These questions are by definition general; you need to have an understanding of the whole passage and the thrust of the argument in order to know what the primary purpose is. Primary purpose questions test your ability to identify the author's perspective and the overall argument. You're not looking through the passage for specific information but instead you need to be able to have a good idea of the author's perspective and their motivation behind expressing it. These questions are part of the same broad group as the main point questions since you're looking to figure out what the author thinks, in this case not the conclusion of the overall argument in the passage but the motivation behind making that argument. Like the main point questions these are general and require evaluation and interpretation of the overall argument.

Approach

Having an understanding of the author's main point and the structure of the overall passage is key. First, you need to come up with the author's main point and overall structure of the passage from the author's perspective. Determine the overall logical relationships in the text and if there's a main point question use it to evaluate the choices. Then, go through the choices and see whether the first part of the choice fits with the tone, structure, and intent of the author's perspective and whether the second part fits with the contents of the author's perspective. The question is general so you won't be evaluating the information in the choice against a specific piece of text but instead against your interpretation of the text as a whole.

Right answer/wrong answer

The correct answer choice correctly identifies the author's motivation and approach, and correctly summarizes the content of the author's perspective. The author's approach and motivation vary from being supportive, critical, or neutral. The incorrect answer choices will misrepresent the author's motivation and approach, and/or the content of the author's perspective. The choices may infer too much or the wrong thing concerning the author's motivation or may focus too narrowly, broadly, or incorrectly on the author's topic.

Summary

The basic approach is to have an understanding of the author's main point along with the structure of the passage and the author's argument and to keep that in mind as you're evaluating the choices for scope and content. These questions are almost always found after main point questions so you can use the answer from the main point question as your guide and vice versa.

6.11 - Inference Questions

Basic info

'It can be inferred from the passage that the author would most likely agree with which one of the following statements?', 'Which one of the following can be most reasonably inferred from the passage?', 'The passage most clearly suggests that the author believes which one of the following?', 'With which one of the following statements would the author most probably agree?', 'According to information in the passage, a widow in early thirteenth-century England could control more land than did her eldest son if ...'

Look for 'inferred' or 'suggests' but be careful since other question types use those terms, particularly 'inferred'. Likewise, an inference question may simply ask what has to be true in the passage. These questions appear frequently, often more than once per passage; and they range from general to specific, though more on the general side. You're tested on your comprehension and ability to make connections and see what has to be true. You're not tested on your memory, won't be hunting through the text for the answer. These questions are quite similar to inference/must be true questions in the arguments section; main difference is that, of course, you're not always going to be dealing with such a short segment. As in the arguments section you're basically looking for an assumption or implication of a piece of information in the passage, or a combination of several pieces of information. The more specific questions will deal with a narrower range of sentences while the more general questions can include the entire passage and will ask for broad generalizations

Approach

It's important to analyze the answer choices. Depending on whether the question is more general or more specific you'll be dealing with more information; for the questions that are more general it's impractical to analyze the entire passage so analyzing the choices is even more important

First determine the scope of the question – is it more specific or more general. If it's specific then determine which part of the passage you need to restrict your attention to and determine what it's talking about. If it's general then keep in mind the paragraph summaries you've been coming up with and the main point. The question may introduce an element that you think leads you to a particular part of the passage but be careful since one of the ways that the testmakers trick you is by causing you to concentrate on an irrelevant part of the passage. Then, move on to the answer choices and evaluate them by eliminating the ones that can't be true. Whether you're dealing with more specific of more general questions; as in the arguments section, the choices that add information, that don't have to be true, that are contrary to information in the passage, or that deal with subtle shifts in terms are incorrect. Negate the choice and look to see if there's a contradiction with anything in the passage; if there's a contradiction then that's the correct choice and if there's no contradiction then it's incorrect.

Right answer/wrong answer

Correct information will provide information that has to be true given the information in the passage. An inference will generally take the form of a synthesis or combination of different pieces of information from the passage, a restatement of a piece of information, or a consequence/necessary condition of a piece of information. Something that has to be true can't be falsified, so when you take the negative of an inference there will be a contradiction with some piece of information in the passage. No essential difference between more specific and more general pieces of information; more general questions take more time because you have to look at more information whereas for the specific questions you're restricted to a smaller area

Incorrect answers will not provide information that has to be true. Any new information means that the choice is incorrect since new information doesn't correspond to anything in the passage and there's no way of knowing if it has to be true; pay attention to shifts in terms. Choices that could be true instead of having to be true are also wrong; pay attention to quantifier adjectives such as 'many', 'some', 'most' etc. There will also be opposite choices – information that can't be true; something that doesn't have to be true can be falsified, so when you take the negative of the choice there won't be a contradiction with any piece of information in the passage. Once again, no essential difference between more specific and more general questions

Summary

Basic approach to doing these questions is to have a good idea of whether the question is asking you to look at a specific area of the passage or the passage in general and then to spend time evaluating the choices to see which one has to be true. You don't have to take the negative of every answer choice but it helps a lot with the one that you think is the correct answer and with any that you're not sure about.

6.12 - Direct Info Questions

Basic info

'According to the passage, which one of the following has to be true?', 'According to the passage, subjectivists advance which one of the following claims to support their charge that objectivism is faulty?', 'Which one of the following is mentioned in the passage as a reason why a married woman might have fulfilled certain duties associated with holding feudal land in thirteenth-century England', etc.

Look for words 'according to passage' or 'mentioned in the passage', etc. Won't find words 'infer' or 'suggest'. These questions appear often, generally at least once per passage and tend to be more specific; they tend to be less difficult because for the most part you're searching for the answer in the passage. You're tested on your ability to isolate relevant information; You're going to be asked to analyze a specific element of the text and choose a piece of information that's important to it in some way. These questions are part of a broad group that includes the inference questions. There is no absolutely clear-cut dividing line between direct info and inference questions; the difference is that direct info questions are more specific and tend to require less inference and interpretation – you'll be doing less restating and combining of different pieces of information and more searching for relevant information.

Approach

The question is the important thing to analyze; you need to carefully analyze it to see what elements it's talking about and what information it's looking for. The first step is to evaluate the question; what are the elements that the question is talking about?, what is the question asking you to look for? The second step is to determine which part of the text you need to focus your attention on and evaluate the choices one by one eliminating the ones that don't correctly represent what's in the passage. The elements that the question introduces will generally restrict your analysis to a specific part of the passage but the answer choices themselves will also suggest a part of the text that you need to look at. The key is to identify the answer choice that states what you find in the passage

Right answer/wrong answer

The correct choice will provide information that presents what's stated in the text; it will generally rephrase text that's found near the information of concern. The correct choices may also be inferences. The incorrect choice will provide information that doesn't present what's stated in the text; the wrong answers will be similar to wrong answers for the inference questions – they'll be new information, irrelevant, contrary, combinations of elements that don't answer the question, etc.

Summary

The basic approach is similar to inference questions the difference being that you're going to be narrower in your scope in terms of what you're looking for and the correct answers will tend to be more restatements or rephrasings as opposed to inferences though inferences do appear; pay attention to what the question brings up and what it asks.

6.13 - Method of Reasoning Questions

Basic info

'The phrase "in England" (lines 30-31) does which one of the following?', 'The author discusses the work of scientists in lines 7-14 primarily to', 'The author's specific purpose in detailing typical talk-story forms (lines 43-51) is to', etc.

The question will present an element from the text and ask what its function is, it may include the word 'purpose' but don't get it confused with the primary purpose questions since you're not being asked for the overall purpose of the passage but for the purpose of only part of it. Method of reasoning questions are fairly common; they appear in the questions for virtually every passage. These questions aren't very difficult since you're directed to the part of the text with the relevant information and you're essentially doing an analysis of the argument, and they're by definition specific. You're asked to evaluate the role that an element plays in an argument in a certain area of the text. You're essentially tested on your ability to analyze the structure of an argument; you're going to be asked to determine the role that an element plays in a certain part of the text. These questions are roughly identical to method of reasoning questions in the arguments section. The major difference is that it's not as obvious what the element is a part of and you have to look through the text carefully to figure out why the author uses that element.

Approach

Most important thing is to figure out what part of the text the element is a part of. You need to be able to determine the relationships within that part of the text and how that part relates to the argument as a whole. First, determine what part of the text the question is asking you to analyze and figure the nature of the relationships within it and how it relates to the passage as a whole. For the most part you'll only need to skim the paragraph that contains the element that you're asked to evaluate, figure out its role in the overall argument, and then you'll need to read carefully the immediate information around the element. Then, come up with a potential function for the element and evaluate it against the answer choices. This is where your evaluation of the structure of the passage as you read through it will be useful.

Right answer/wrong answer

The correct answer will most accurately describe the role played by the element in the question and will correctly identify its relationship to other statements in the immediate area. The incorrect answer will misidentify the role of the element or its relationship to the relevant area of the text. The choice might say that the element supports when it refutes, etc and it might tie it to information that isn't related to it.

Summary

Basic approach is to have an idea of what the relationships are in the area of the text where the element in the question is found.

6.14 - Meaning Questions

'Which one of the following most accurately expresses the meaning of the word "sway" as it is used in line 60 of the passage?', 'It can be inferred from the passage that the author uses the phrase "personally remembered stories" (line 32) primarily to refer to', etc.

The question will always present a word or phrase/concept and the place in the text where it's located. These questions don't appear often but you'll find them in every test once every two or three passages; they're not very difficult, the answer is in the passage and you're told where to look. And they're specific. You're tested on your ability to use context to figure out the meaning of relevant terms. You're going to be given a term and asked to identify the choice that best defines it. These questions are part of the broad group that includes inference and direct info. This group of questions basically ask you to go back to the passage and find information that has to be true; they emphasize research and interpretation and meaning questions are the most specific.

Having good understanding of context and argument in text is key. The first step is to go back to the passage and determine context and usage as best you can. Roughly speaking read from five lines before the term is mentioned to five lines after it's mentioned or from is a natural beginning to a natural end. Next, evaluate the answer choices by seeing whether they match with the meaning you came up with or with what's in the passage. Look at the key concepts that the answer choice introduces and see if that fits with what's in the passage. The correct choices will use concepts that are relevant to the term in the text and incorrect choices will add information, be irrelevant, subtly shift the terms, etc.

Right answer/wrong answer

The correct answer choice will define the term in accordance with the context and usage where the terms if found. The way the term or phrase is used is going to correspond to the key concepts that the answer choice introduces. The incorrect answer choice will provide a definition that is at odds with the context and usage in the passage. The key concepts that the choice introduces will not be relevant to the context and usage in the text, they'll generally either be new information or referencing other parts of the text, subtle shifts in meaning, etc.

Summary

This question doesn't have an analog in the arguments section but it's within the same basic group as the inference and direct info questions in that you're analyzing the text to see which of the answer choices has to be true. This question type is much more specific than the other two tend to be.

6.15 - Analogy Questions

'Based on the passage, which one of the following is most clearly an instance of the objectivist approach to studying the mind?', 'Which one of the following is most closely analogous to the debate described in the hypothetical example given by the author in the fourth paragraph?', 'In which one of the following is the use of cotton fibers or cotton cloth most analogous to Kingston's use of the English language as described in lines 51-55?'

The question will most likely include the word 'analogous' or 'analogy' but not necessarily. The answer choices will contain information on a topic that isn't in the passage. These questions appear relatively frequently, once every couple of passages and they tend to be more specific than general and they will ask you to look at a more or less narrow area of the text to find the corresponding analogy in the choices. Analogy questions test your ability to understand the more abstract relationships between information and concepts presented in the text. You're going to be given answer choices that deal with topics not mentioned in the text and the point is to figure out which ones are parallel to the information in the text at an abstract level. These questions are similar to the principle scenario questions in the arguments section; you generally won't be dealing with arguments in these questions but instead with areas of the text that develop a certain concept or element of the overall argument.

Most important thing is to have a good understanding of what the question is asking you to find the analogy for. You won't be able to come up with a potential answer but you'll need a good understanding of what you're being asked about in order to evaluate the choices. First, evaluate the element that you're being asked to find an analogy to; think about how it's presented and defined, and what its function is within the passage as a whole. Come up with an abstract definition/description that breaks down the element into different parts. Then, go through the answer choices one by one and evaluate to see which one is most parallel to what you've established about the element in the question. The information in the choices will be new and off-topic; you're looking to see if the abstract relationships are analogous.

Right answer/wrong answer

The right answers will provide something that fits the abstractions developed for the elements from the question. The different parts of the element in the text will be parallel with the parts of the analogous scenario in the answer choice. The wrong answers will not capture the correct relationships and abstractions. Some of the wrong answers may seem tempting because they may deal with information that's similar to the information in the text, but the content isn't what's important, it's the relationships behind the content that are important.

Summary

Basic approach is to have a good idea of what the question is asking you about – to define and describe it and pay attention to how it's related to the rest of the passage and then use that information to evaluate the answer choices one by one paying attention to the abstractions and not the content of the choices.

6.16 - Strengthen/Weaken Questions

Basic info

'Which one of the following, if true, would most clearly undermine a portion of Ringer's argument as the argument is described in the passage?', 'Which one of the following, if true, would lend the most credence to the author's statement in lines 55 – 59?', etc. Question will include words like 'undermine', 'weaken', 'support', 'strengthen', etc.

Strengthen and weaken questions are fairly rare, they appear least of all the question types we've gone over – once every three or four passages; these questions range in difficulty. Both strengthen and weaken questions range from more specific to encompassing the passage as a whole. You're tested on your ability to evaluate the strength and support for arguments or assertions in the text. These questions are virtually identical to 'weaken' and 'strengthen' questions in the arguments section. The major difference of course is that it's not as obvious what the argument that you're evaluating is because it's embedded within the passage as a whole.

Approach

The most important thing for both strengthen and weaken questions is to have a good idea of what you're being asked to strengthen or weaken and what the support for it is. The first thing is to determine what the question is asking you to evaluate. If it's a general question then determine what the author's conclusion is and what the overall argument is. If it's a specific question then determine what the argument is in the part of the text that's specified. Then, go through the answer choices and see which one weakens or strengthens the point in question, depending on the question. In either case you have to make sure that the information in the answer choice is relevant to the argument in the text. If the question asks for the choice that weakens then you have to pick the one that makes the conclusion of the argument or the certainty of the assertion less likely. If the question asks for the choice that strengthens then you have to pick the one that makes the conclusion of the argument or the certainty of the assertion more likely.

Right answer/wrong answer

Strengthen :

As with the strengthen questions in the arguments section the correct answers will provide information that makes the conclusion or the certainty of the assertion referenced in the question more likely. The choice might be new information that independently provides support or it might make explicit key missing information or it might make less likely something that would weaken the conclusion or assertion. And likewise as with the argument strengthen questions the incorrect answer will not provide support. But that doesn't mean that it will weaken, just that it may simply be irrelevant, though of course it could also weaken. Wrong choices will also often attack something that seems to be related but is in fact only seemingly related.

weaken:

As with the weaken argument questions the correct answers will provide information that undermines the conclusion or the assertion. The correct choice will generally not directly contradict something in the text but it will provide additional information that makes the point in the conclusion less likely. The incorrect answer will not undermine the conclusion or the assertion. This doesn't mean that it will strengthen, it may, but it may also simply be irrelevant. Wrong choices will also often attack something that seems to be related but is in fact only superficially related.

summary

The basic approach is to have a good idea of what the overall argument is or the support for the point in the question and to pay attention to the relevance of the answer choices.

6.17 - Dual Passage Questions

Although you will be asked to answer a question that involves only one of the two passages, most of the questions will deal with both passages. There are two common variations to the dual passages. In one variation, the passages are evaluated as separate and distinct and you are in some way comparing and contrasting them. And in the other variation, the passages are evaluated as parts of a coherent whole and you're in some way analyzing their relationship.

Questions dealing with one passage

These questions are analogous to the questions for the other kinds of passages in the reading comprehension section. They will always identify which passage you need to look at and they will generally deal with the main point, inference, or direct info types of questions, as well as other types.

ie:

"Which one of the following most accurately expresses the main point of passage A?"

"Which one of the following claims about the Roma is NOT made in passage A?"

Questions dealing with both passages, where the passages are separate and discrete

For these questions you'll need to read through both passages and consider their similarities and differences without thinking about how to integrate their content into some sort of whole. In a variation of this subtype you'll be asked to identify some sort of coherence or agreement.

ie:

- **"Both passages explicitly mention which one of the following?"**

- **"Each of the passages contains information sufficient to answer which one of the following questions?"**

- "It can be inferred that both authors would be most likely to agree with which one of the following statements?"

- "The term 'problematic' has which one of the following meanings in both passage A (line 19) and passage B (line 35)?"

- "'Which one of the following is a principle that can be most reasonably considered to underlie the reasoning in both of the passages?"

In yet another variation you will be asked to identify some sort of conflict or disagreement.

ie:

- "It can be inferred that the authors would be most likely to disagree with which one of the following?"

- "Which one of the following, if true, would cast doubt on the argument in passage B but bolster the argument in passage A?"

- "In which one of the following ways are the passages NOT parallel?"

- "Which one of the following is discussed in passage B but not in passage A?"

- "Each of the following is supported by one or both of the passages EXCEPT:"

Questions dealing with both passages, where the passages are part of an integrated whole

For these questions you'll need to pay attention to how the two passages are related to one another and what the encompassing themes are that incorporate the information from both the passages. These questions will generally ask about the relationship between the two passages or about a specific aspect of the relationship.

ie:

- "Which one of the following is true about the relationship between the two passages?"

- "The relationship between which one of the following pairs of documents is most analogous to the relationship between passage A and passage B?"

- "If the author of passage A were to read passage B, he or she would be most likely to agree with which one of the following?"

- "Which one of the following most accurately describes the attitude expressed by the author of passage B toward the overall argument represented by passage A?"

- "Which one of the following can be most reasonably inferred from the two passages taken together, but not from either one individually?"

To do the questions that incorporate both passages you will need to pay attention to the ways in which the information in the two passages is similar or different across passages as well as how each passages as a whole is related to the other. Since the questions are basically the same questions as the ones we've covered for the regular passages, the approaches will in essence be the same.

7

Final Note - Appendix

I hope that this ebook was useful and that you are now better equipped to tackle the LSAT. If you would like more in-depth coverage of the topics covered or are thinking of getting tutoring please visit my website for more info.

In this appendix I've arranged information that you might find useful, such as questions lists and useful links.

A1 - Logic Games Questions from 1st 10 Tests

arrangement can be true questions

LSAT	section	questions
7	2	19
9	3	1, 8
10	2	12, 13, 19
11	1	1, 12, 23
13	1	1, 12
14	1	1, 13
15	4	1, 14
16	1	1, 19
18	1	1, 7, 20

can be true questions

LSAT	section	questions
7	2	3, 9, 11, 13, 24
9	3	7, 15, 2, 3, 9, 14, 15
10	2	2, 3, 9, 14, 15
11	1	2, 3, 4, 8, 10, 13, 17, 21, 22
12	2	2, 5, 7, 18, 19, 20, 22
13	1	4, 9, 13, 14, 17, 18, 19, 24

14	1	3, 4, 8, 11, 14, 22, 24
15	4	5, 15, 19, 20, 21
16	1	8, 11, 14, 15, 16, 21, 22, 24
18	1	2, 5, 9, 10, 13, 15

must be false questions

LSAT	section	questions
7	2	2
9	3	10
10	2	5, 10, 20, 21, 24
11	1	6, 7, 9, 16
12	2	10
13	1	5, 6, 7, 15, 23
14	1	7, 10, 12, 17, 20, 23
15	4	6, 18
16	1	4, 13
18	1	8

must be true questions

LSAT	section	questions
7	2	1, 4, 7, 8, 10, 12, 14, 15, 16, 20, 21, 23
9	3	4, 5, 6, 9, 11, 13, 16, 17, 18
10	2	4, 6, 7, 22, 23
11	1	5, 11, 14, 15, 18, 19, 20, 24
12	2	1, 4, 8, 9, 10, 11, 12, 15, 16, 21, 23, 24
13	1	2, 3, 10, 11, 16, 20, 21, 22
14	1	2, 5, 15, 16, 18, 19, 21
15	4	2, 3, 4, 16, 17, 22, 23, 24
16	1	3, 5, 6, 7, 9, 10, 12, 17, 23
18	1	3, 6, 11, 12, 23

can be false questions

LSAT	section	questions
7	2	18
16	1	20
18	1	4

list questions

LSAT	section	questions
7	2	17 (except), 22
9	3	14
10	2	8, 11, 17
12	2	3, 6
13	1	8
14	1	9 (except)
16	1	2, 18 (except)

greatest/smallest questions

LSAT	section	questions
7	2	5, 6
9	3	2, 3
10	2	16, 18
12	2	13, 14, 17
18	1	24

diagram questions

LSAT	section	questions
9	3	12
10	2	1

A2 - Arguments Questions from 1st 10 Tests

conclusion, strengthen, weaken questions

conclusion questions	weaken questions	strengthen questions
LSAT 7	LSAT 7	LSAT 7
Section 1: question 9	Section 1: questions 1, 4	Section 1: questions 15, 23
Section 4: questions 2, 7, 10	Section 4: question 4	Section 4: questions 1, 18
LSAT 9	LSAT 9	LSAT 9
Section 2: question 3	Section 2: questions 4, 5, 7, 12	Section 2: questions 9, 10
Section 4: question 18	Section 4: questions 2, 22	Section 4: question 17
LSAT 10		LSAT 10
Section 1: questions 11, 24	LSAT 10	Section 1: question 9
Section 4: questions 3, 10, 22	Section 1: questions 16, 19	Section 4: questions 2, 11
LSAT 11	Section 4: questions 1, 9, 14	LSAT 11
Section 2: question 4	LSAT 11	Section 4: questions 18
Section 4: questions 8, 14, 16	Section 2: questions 1, 11, 19, 21	LSAT 12
LSAT 12	Section 4: questions 5, 9, 11, 21	Section 1: questions 11, 15, 19
Section 1: questions 1, 9	LSAT 12	LSAT 13
Section 4: questions 10, 3	Section 1: questions	Section 2: question 5

LSAT 13

Section 4: question 3

LSAT 14

Section 2: questions 14, 19, 23

LSAT 15

Section 2: questions 8, 11

Section 3: questions 1, 4, 19

LSAT 16

Section 3: question 19

LSAT 18

Section 2: questions 10, 18

Section 4: question 2

16, 24

Section 4: questions 4, 11, 13, 21

LSAT 13

Section 2: questions 1, 13, 21

Section 4: questions 12, 17, 19, 20

LSAT 14

Section 2: questions 12, 21, 24

Section 4: questions 4, 6, 22, 25

LSAT 15

Section 2: question 7

Section 3: question 25

LSAT 16

Section 2: questions 2, 5, 16

Section 3: questions 1, 6, 18

LSAT 18

Section 2: questions 4, 7

Section 4: questions 14, 23

Section 4: question 23

LSAT 14

Section 2: questions 6, 7

LSAT 15

Section 2: question 3

Section 3: questions 8, 10, 23

LSAT 16

Section 2: questions 18, 21

Section 3: question 13

LSAT 18

Section 2: questions 16, 21

Section 4: question 5

assumption, logical conclusion, evaluate questions

assumption questions	logical conclusion questions	evaluate questions
LSAT 7	LSAT 7	LSAT 7
Section 1: questions 14, 24	Section 1: questions 2, 5	Section 1: question 22
Section 4: questions 6, 24	Section 4: questions 13, 23	Section 4: question 8
LSAT 9	LSAT 9	LSAT 9
Section 2: questions 19, 21, 25	Section 2: question 23	Section 4: question 8
Section 4: questions 6, 10, 25	Section 4: questions 12, 19	LSAT 10
LSAT 10	LSAT 11	Section 4: question 6
Section 1: questions 1, 3, 7	Section 2: question 22	LSAT 11
Section 4: questions 4, 8, 18	LSAT 12	Section 2: question 2
LSAT 11	Section 1: question 22	LSAT 13
Section 2: questions 5, 13, 15, 18, 24	Section 4: questions 8, 20	Section 2: question 22
Section 4: questions 7, 13, 15	LSAT 13	Section 4: question 23
LSAT 12	Section 2: question 9	LSAT 14
Section 1: questions 2, 10, 13	LSAT 14	Section 2: questions 6, 7
Section 4: questions 2, 6	Section 2: questions 13, 17	Section 4: questions
	Section 4: questions 1, 7, 23	LSAT 15
		Section 2: question 22
		Section 3: questions 16, 22

LSAT 13

Section 2: questions 12, 14

Section 4: questions 4, 8, 11, 18, 20

LSAT 14

Section 2: question 18

Section 4: questions 13, 19

LSAT 15

Section 2: questions 6, 16, 23

Section 3: questions 3, 12, 24

LSAT 16

Section 2: questions 6, 14

Section 3: questions 3, 12, 14

LSAT 18

Section 2: questions 3, 9, 15

Section 4: questions 8, 18, 22

LSAT 15

Section 3: question 18

LSAT 18

Section 2: question 2

Section 4: question 12

principle (justify) and principle (scenario) questions

principle (justify) questions	principle (scenario) questions
LSAT 7	LSAT 9
Section 4: question 5	Section 2: question 18
LSAT 9	LSAT 10
Section 4: questions 11, 21	Section 1: question 23
LSAT 10	LSAT 13
Section 1: questions 6, 15	Section 4: question 2, 16
LSAT 11	LSAT 14
Section 2: questions 6, 10	Section 2: question 2
Section 4: question 6	LSAT 16
LSAT 12	Section 2: question 8
Section 1: question 5	LSAT 18
Section 4: question 18	Section 4: question 19
LSAT 13	
Section 2: question 16	
Section 4: question 22	
LSAT 14	
Section 2: questions 14, 19, 23	
LSAT 15	
Section 2: questions 1, 13, 21	
Section 3: question 6	

LSAT 16

Section 2: question 12

Section 3: question 23

LSAT 18

Section 2: question 24

Section 4: questions 1, 16

inference, can't be true, and formal logic questions

inference questions	can't be true questions	formal logic questions
LSAT 7	LSAT 7	LSAT 7
Section 1: questions 8, 16, 21	Section 1: question 19	Section 1: question 12
Section 4: questions 15, 19	Section 4: question 12	LSAT 9
LSAT 9	LSAT 9	Section 2: questions 16, 23
Section 2: question 13	Section 2: question 17	LSAT 11
Section 4: questions 4, 7, 13, 16, 23	LSAT 13	Section 2: questions 7, 12
LSAT 10	Section 4: question 21	LSAT 12
Section 1: questions 18, 22	LSAT 18	Section 1: question 25
Section 4: questions 16, 20, 24	Section 2: question 23	LSAT 13
		Section 2: question 10
		Section 4: question 14

LSAT 11

Section 2: question 16

Section 4: question 4

LSAT 12

Section 1: questions 8, 21

Section 4: questions 1, 3, 16

LSAT 13

Section 2: questions 4, 6, 18, 25

Section 4: questions 5, 14, 18

LSAT 14

Section 2: questions 11, 16

Section 4: questions 5, 17, 21

LSAT 15

Section 2: questions 9, 12, 15

Section 3: questions 5, 7, 21, 26

LSAT 16

Section 2: questions 3, 9, 11, 20

Section 3: questions 5,

LSAT 18

Section 2: question 2

8, 16, 21

LSAT 18

Section 2: question 20

Section 4: questions 6, 10, 24

paradox and disagreement questions

paradox questions	disagreement questions
LSAT 7	LSAT 10
Section 1: questions 11, 25	Section 4: question 7
Section 4: question 17	LSAT 13
LSAT 9	Section 2: question 11
Section 2: questions 6, 8	Section 4: question 7
Section 4: question 3	LSAT 14
LSAT 10	Section 4: questions 11, 12
Section 1: questions 2, 14	LSAT 16
Section 4: questions 17, 23	Section 2: question 13
LSAT 11	Section 3: question 4
Section 2: question 23	
Section 4: question 1	
LSAT 12	

Section 1: questions 4, 7, 12

Section 4: questions 12, 22

LSAT 13

Section 2: questions 3, 15, 19

Section 4: question 2, 10, 13

LSAT 14

Section 2: questions 1, 3, 5

Section 4: question 3

LSAT 15

Section 2: questions 5, 10

Section 3: question 20

LSAT 16

Section 2: questions 1, 4, 15

Section 3: questions 10, 17

LSAT 18

Section 2: questions 11, 19, 22

Section 4: questions 13, 15

method of reasoning, flaw in the argument, and parallel reasoning questions

method of reasoning questions	flaw in the argument questions	parallel reasoning questions
LSAT 7	LSAT 7	LSAT 7
Section 1: questions 6, 7, 18	Section 1: questions 10, 17	Section 1: questions 13, 20
Section 4: questions 16, 20, 21	Section 4: questions 3, 9, 11, 22	Section 4: questions 14, 25
LSAT 9	LSAT 9	LSAT 9
Section 2: questions 11, 15, 20	Section 2: questions 2, 14, 22	Section 2: questions 1, 24
Section 4: questions 9, 20	Section 4: questions 1, 5, 14	Section 4: questions 15, 24
LSAT 10	LSAT 10	LSAT 10
Section 1: questions 4, 12	Section 1: questions 5, 8, 10, 13, 17, 21	Section 1: questions 20, 25
Section 4: questions 13, 25	Section 4: questions 19, 21	Section 4: questions 5, 12
LSAT 11	LSAT 11	LSAT 11
Section 2: questions 3, 8, 14, 20	Section 2: questions 9, 15, 26	Section 2: questions 17, 25
Section 4: questions 2, 10, 12, 24	Section 4: questions 3, 17, 19, 23	Section 4: questions 20, 22
LSAT 12	LSAT 12	LSAT 12
Section 1: questions 3, 6	Section 1: questions 14, 18, 20	Section 1: questions 17, 23
Section 4: question 14	Section 4: questions 5, 7, 15, 17, 19	Section 4: questions 9, 23

LSAT 13

Section 2: questions 2, 17

Section 4: questions 1, 6

LSAT 14

Section 2: questions 8, 9

Section 4: questions 16, 24

LSAT 15

Section 2: questions 14, 24

Section 3: questions 11, 15, 17

LSAT 16

Section 2: questions 17, 23

Section 3: questions 7, 20, 25

LSAT 18

Section 2: questions 1, 5, 7, 12

Section 4: question 21

LSAT 13

Section 2: questions 7, 20, 24, 26

Section 4: question 9

LSAT 14

Section 2: questions 10, 22

Section 4: questions 9, 10, 15, 18, 20

LSAT 15

Section 2: questions 2, 17, 19, 20

Section 3: questions 2, 9, 14, 19

LSAT 16

Section 2: questions 10, 22, 24

Section 3: questions 2, 9, 11, 24, 26

LSAT 18

Section 2: questions 4, 8, 14

Section 4: questions 9, 11, 17, 25

LSAT 13

Section 2: questions 8, 23

Section 4: questions 15, 24

LSAT 14

Section 2: questions 15, 25

Section 4: questions 8, 14

LSAT 15

Section 2: questions 4, 18

Section 3: questions 13, 22

LSAT 16

Section 2: questions 7, 19

Section 3: questions 15, 22

LSAT 18

Section 2: questions 13, 17

Section 4: questions 3, 20

Made in the USA
Columbia, SC
02 August 2024